TERMINAL CARE
IN THE COMMUNITY

A guide for pharmacists

Edited by Barbara J. Stewart

Distance Learning

Radcliffe Medical Press
Oxford

© Copyright Controller of HMSO
1992

'Techniques exist to alleviate the worst miseries of the dying patient and there are also ways in which the family can be helped. This is not a matter of new buildings or expensive equipment. It depends primarily on enlightened professional attitudes.'

From the Report of a Working Group on Terminal Care; Standing Medical Advisory Committee, 1980.

Reprinted 1993

Printed in Great Britain by
T.J. Press (Padstow) Ltd, Padstow, Cornwall.

Contents

List of Contributors   vii

Foreword by Tom West   viii

Preface   ix

1 Introduction   1
  The hospice movement
  Patterns of dying and death
  Models of care
  Hospitals
  Home care services
  Home care and the general practitioner
  The challenge in the community
  Further reading

2 Philosophy of Terminal Illness   9
  Acceptance of the reality of death
  Communication in terminal illness
  The reactions and fears of the dying patient
  Home care
  Caring for the carers
  Ethical issues in terminal illness
  Ethical problems in ethnic groups
  Physiology of dying
  Euthanasia
  Further reading

3 Palliative Care   21
  Symptom control
  Pain

Depression
Nausea and vomiting
Dyspnoea
Constipation
Confusion
Insomnia
Other symptoms
Crisis points
Conclusion
Further reading

4   Pharmaceutical Aspects of Pain Control   49
The analgesic ladder
Morphine and diamorphine
Morphine preparations
Parenteral formulation of diamorphine
Ambulatory infusion devices
Admixtures
Conclusion
References
Further reading

5   Community Pharmacists and Terminal Care   63
A specialised form of the 'extended role'
Identifying terminal patients in the community
Helping to achieve compliance
Using traditional pharmaceutical expertise
Case studies
Professional interaction
Coping with emotional aspects
Communication
Future developments
Further reading

6   Legal Aspects of Controlled Drug Use in Terminal Care   75
Misuse of Drugs Act
Levels of control
Prescriptions
Dispensing
Security
Returned prescriptions

Supplies to hospices
Further advice
References

7 **Cancer Pain Relief and Palliative Care:
An International Perspective** 82
WHO programme
Opioid availability
Risk of diversion
Risk of psychological dependence from medically prescribed
    opioids
Tolerance to opioids
Availability of other drugs for the relief of cancer pain
Networks
Pharmaceutical profession
Hospice pharmacy in the United States of America
Further reading

8 **AIDS and its Implications for Palliative Care** 90
Background to the syndrome
The virus
How the virus is spread
Clinical aspects
Palliative care of AIDS patients
Counselling
Antiviral therapy
Symptom control
Control of infection
Further reading

Appendix A: Information on key organisations 101

Appendix B: Useful addresses of organisations providing help 109
and advice to health care professionals, patients
and their families

Appendix C: Body chart for pain assessment 113

Appendix D: Further aspects of palliative care 115

Appendix E: Bereavement 119

Appendix F: Home chemotherapy; Royal Pharmaceutical   123
Society Working Party Report

Appendix G: General use of the Graseby Syringe Driver   125

Appendix H: Information on courses, videotapes and journals   129
relevant to palliative care

Appendix I: Cancer pain relief and palliative care   133
Report of the WHO Expert Committee
Recommendations to Member States

Index   135

List of Contributors

JAMES HANRATTY OBE, KSG, Chairman and formerly Medical Director, St Joseph's Hospice, Hackney, London.

ROBIN HULL FRCGP, Macmillan Senior Lecturer in Palliative Care, Department of General Practice, Birmingham University Medical School. He has been in general medical practice for many years and written widely about many aspects of palliative care, including the special problems associated with AIDS.

GRAHAM SEWELL BPharm, PhD, MRPharmS, MRSC, MIBiol, Principal Pharmacist and Senior Lecturer in Biomedical Sciences, Department of Pharmacy, Royal Devon and Exeter Hospital. He acts as Scientific Director to the FORCE Cancer Research Centre, Exeter, Devon.

ALAN STEARS, Senior Inspector, Drugs Branch of the Home Office, Leeds.

BARBARA J. STEWART BPharm, MPhil, MRPharmS, Pharmaceutical Consultant and formerly Head of the Education Division of the Royal Pharmaceutical Society. She has been associated with recent initiatives in continuing education for community pharmacists.

TOM WEST OBE, MB BS, Medical Director, St Christopher's Hospice, Sydenham, London.

Foreword

Good palliative care for people suffering from a terminal disease includes improved communication and relevant family support, but it starts with skilful symptom control. Unless pain, dyspnoea and other distressing symptoms are adequately controlled, effective counselling and family involvement will be difficult or impossible.

Pharmacists should be important contributors to the skilful prescribing needed when the many symptoms of terminal disease are being addressed. They will take, I believe, an increasingly important part in the multidisciplinary team approach that is needed for the management of 'Total Pain'.

Pharmacists are particularly well placed to monitor a patient's (and family's) progress over the last weeks and months of life, noting times of crisis and advising appropriately. They may then help to support family members through the time of bereavement, aware that here again there will be occasions when further medical help should be suggested.

I commend *Terminal Care in the Community: a guide for pharmacists* and believe it will be a further step in the integration of pharmacists into the whole caring team.

Dr Tom West, OBE
Medical Director
St Christopher's Hospice
London

February 1992

Preface

This book is written for community pharmacists who have an interest in, or who are actively involved in, the palliative care of terminally ill patients in the community. Whilst the book will stand on its own, it is designed to accompany the video *Terminal Care in the Community: a guide for pharmacists*, which forms part of an educational programme funded by the Department of Health specifically for community pharmacists.

Many pharmacists will have encountered terminally ill patients or their families at some time, although the experience and skills gained in dealing with this special category of patients will be varied. Some will have had little opportunity to learn outside their practice setting or have had access to educational material relevant to community pharmacy. This book is designed primarily for this group of pharmacists, although pharmacists from a variety of practice settings should find it instructive.

The Terminal Care Programme sets out to fulfil the educational needs of pharmacists who find themselves involved in the care of terminally ill patients and their families at home. The aims of the programme are:

- to enhance understanding of the concepts involved in this special form of patient care;
- to assist in increasing knowledge of common symptoms and their management;
- to provide information on improved methods of palliative care;
- to raise psychological insight into communication with patients and carers.

The authors have been drawn from medical and pharmaceutical practice, and from other disciplines in an attempt to achieve a broad and balanced perspective. Gratitude is extended to the many people and organisations who have contributed willingly to the programme, including community pharmacists Mary Box of Sydenham, London and Michael Chapman of Taunton, Somerset; Sue Tempest, senior clinical pharmacist in palliative and emergency medicine (Derbyshire Royal

Infirmary); St Christopher's Hospice; the Marie Curie Foundation; Help
the Hospices; and the Home Office.

Barbara J. Stewart
February 1992

1   Introduction

Barbara J. Stewart

The hospice movement

In the last 25 years great advances have been made in the care of the
terminally ill. The majority of these advances are due to the work of the
hospices, and health workers like Dame Cicely Saunders. When Dame
Cicely established St Christopher's Hospice in 1967 the aim was to
provide a place not only where effective care could be given to the
terminally ill but also where research and teaching could take place. St
Christopher's became the catalyst and the model for hospice care both in
the United Kingdom and the United States. The philosophy of hospice
care has now spread to more than 40 countries, breaking both political
and religious boundaries. The philosophy has been to offer the patient a
service tailored towards palliative rather than curative care, an
acceptance of dignified death and a focus on the psychological and social
needs of the patient and his or her family. Although originally
established for the care of patients with cancer, hospices usually also
accept patients with motor neurone disease and today some are
beginning to accept patients with AIDS. Over the next few years the
remit for hospices will probably increase. The role model of the hospice
is of fundamental importance when considering any form of palliative
care of terminally ill patients, and should be understood even if one is
mainly involved in care in the community.

Terminal care services are distributed unevenly throughout the
country. In England, terminal care beds are mainly provided by
independent hospices. A typical hospice probably has:

- inpatient facilities for the terminally ill;
- respite care beds;
- home care team;
- day centre;
- bereavement service;

- teaching service;
- hospital advisory service.

The home care team provides the hospice with an outreach into the community. In partnership with the primary care team, the home care team supports the terminally ill patient and his or her family at home, as well as those patients who return home following admission to a hospice. Community pharmacists are most likely to come into contact with members of home care teams.

The establishment of *day centres* within hospices is a recent development. Their function is to provide a day out for patients living at home and a day off for the caring relatives. Patients usually attend a day centre once or twice a week.

Hospices are much involved in *teaching* on terminal care, death and bereavement. The level of involvement depends on local needs and resources, can include seminars, lectures, symposia and, where appropriate, clinical attachments.

The philosophical and theoretical basis for hospice care is the nursing model, whereas much health care in society is based on the traditional medical model of care. The nursing and modern medical model of care emphasises the whole person, the inclusion of the family and maximising the patient's quality of life. The emphasis should be on meeting patients' and their families' needs effectively, rather than on maintaining professional boundaries. The hospice approach does not deny the fact of death but ensures that all aspects preceding it receive attention and care. The main aim of those providing terminal care should be to improve the quality of remaining life.

AIDS

Hospice policy towards patients with AIDS is determined separately by each hospice. At present there is a small number of hospices committed to the care of AIDS patients alone, (e.g. the Mildmay Hospice, Hackney, London) while several more are in the process of being set up. People with AIDS usually prefer to remain in the community, therefore the extension of the hospice philosophy into AIDS care is being achieved through specific home care teams for AIDS patients (*see* Chapter 8).

Patterns of death and dying

Modern culture has decreased our awareness of the dying process and the medicalisation of death has largely removed the concept of 'natural death'. At present, 56% of all deaths in England and Wales occur in hospital. At a local level, the number of urban deaths occurring in hospital is nearer 70%, whereas in rural areas the majority of deaths occur in the patient's home. Recent improvements in medical techniques, together with developments in community care, have considerably reduced the length of time dying patients actually spend in hospitals. For the most part, patients will be cared for at home with a final admission of only a few days. The majority of patients would prefer to die comfortably at home and their wishes should be respected.

Different patterns of care for the dying exist but all should allow patients to die with dignity. The decision to change from curative to palliative therapy can present the medical profession with a complex moral and ethical dilemma. In keeping the patient comfortable and as free from pain as possible, the benefits from treatment aimed at the relief of symptoms are enormous.

Estimates of the need for terminal care are difficult to assess. The period of survival in a terminal state is highly variable. A large number of people die from cancer, for example in 1989 a quarter of all deaths in the United Kingdom were attributed to some form of malignant neoplasm. Also, the expanding population of elderly people has important implications on the planning of terminal care services. A move towards home-based care and allowances for death to take place at home where possible, will require consideration of the fact that a substantial and increasing proportion of the elderly live alone.

Models of care

There are various models of care for the terminally ill, as illustrated in Fig. 1.1. (overleaf)

Hospitals

Hospital admittances are generally the result of a combination of three main factors: inability to control symptoms; lack of family members or friends to care for dying patients in their home; and lack of Social Service support. Patients may sometimes attend a hospital as an outpatient following a period as an inpatient.

The hospice approach has been introduced into acute hospitals through the establishment of Hospital Support Teams. The teams work in an advisory capacity within the hospital providing symptom control, pain relief and emotional support to patients, families and staff, as well as playing an important role in education within the hospital. Most teams comprise two or more nurses and many teams are multidisciplinary. Some teams also supplement care within the community by maintaining contact with outpatients.

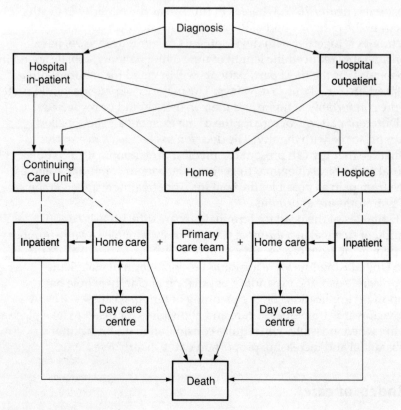

Figure 1.1   Patterns of care for the terminally ill. Reproduced from: *Dying with Dignity*, Office of Health Economics, London

Some NHS hospitals have designated wards or units specifically for palliative care. In some cases, part of the funding for conversion or building such wards has been provided by independent charities including the Cancer Relief Macmillan Fund.

Macmillan cancer care units

Some hospitals have palliative care units which were initially funded by the Cancer Relief Macmillan Fund and built in the grounds of NHS hospitals. At present there are 12 Macmillan continuing care units, each with between 15 and 25 beds. The units are now funded and run by the NHS. Day facilities are also available within the units.

Hospices

Around 113 independent hospices which are registered charities, provide inpatient, home care and day care services. Two national charitable organisations, the Marie Curie Memorial Foundation and the Sue Ryder Foundation also contribute. Residential care is provided at 11 Marie Curie Cancer Care centres, some with home care teams attached, while a Community Nursing Service operates nationally. Sue Ryder Homes provide inpatient care for patients with a wide range of disabilities.

Home care services

For many patients a home care service may be more appropriate, enabling them to remain at home with their families and supported by the local home care team, which works closely with the patient's general practitioner (GP) and the primary health care team. There are presently about 360 home care teams in the United Kingdom and Ireland, of which about 137 are attached to hospice inpatient units. Most home care teams are funded by the Cancer Relief Macmillan Fund and take the name Macmillan Nursing Service. The service provides specially trained nurses to advise on pain and symptom control and to give emotional support to patients and their families. Referral may be through the patient's GP or hospital consultant. The nurses also work alongside the primary community health care team.

Marie Curie Cancer Care provides and funds a similar home care service from 9 of its 11 centres. A Community Nursing Service is also provided in partnership with the local District Nursing Service in most Health Authorities and in association with other independent hospices. The main demand is for night nursing to relieve those caring at home.

Day hospices

Day care is now a major part of the hospice movement, allowing patients to both live at home and keep in contact with all hospice facilities. A wide range of creative and social activities is provided, as well as physiotherapy, occupational therapy, hairdressing, chiropody and beauty treatments. Approximately 180 day hospices exist, either free standing or attached to hospice inpatient units or teams.

Home care and the general practitioner

Because of recent improvements in medical techniques and developments in community care, patients are cared for at home, with a final admission to hospital of only a few days. Under the supervision of the patient's GP and with the support of the primary health care nursing team, successful home care can undoubtedly produce good terminal care. Many families wish to look after a dying relative if at all possible and gain the satisfaction and comfort from doing so – but not every patient's circumstances are such that adequate care and facilities can be provided. Different illnesses make different demands on relatives. In addition, in some districts the level of staffing in the primary care sector may be insufficient to provide the level of care necessary. The willingness of the GP to undertake such care is an essential factor.

It is essential to ensure that adequate symptom and pain relief is available whenever it is needed. The family will need to know that if problems arise they can contact their GP or a trusted and known community nurse in the evening or during the night. As well as managing symptom control, the GP has an important additional role as coordinator of the various sources of help. The evolution of a specialist community-based service, referred to below, enables the primary care team to maintain their traditional clinical role, with referral to specialists where appropriate. Various facilities exist to supplement the domestic circumstances of the patient. Local Authority Social Services can provide home-helps, laundry services and various aids to living.

Dealing with terminally ill patients and families can be stressful. Extremes of emotional reaction are very difficult to cope with. Patients come from a variety of cultural, religious and social backgrounds, which can make an interpretation of their reactions more difficult, particularly if language barriers exist. Also, patients may not volunteer questions if the GP appears busy or uninterested. Practitioners should be sensitive to the effects of their verbal and non-verbal communication with patients. (Communication is discussed further in Chapters 2, 3 and 5).

The social worker is often in a position to stand back from the medical and nursing aspects of patient care and provide important counselling (and later bereavement support), plus advice on financial support for the patient and family. In addition, primary health care teams need to build relationships with spiritual advisers. The importance of learning about the variety of cultural and religious needs of patients is described in Chapter 2. The special perspective of the clergy can restore some of the normality and significance of death and grief.

The challenge in the community

In the primary care setting, the combination of severe illness and emotional difficulties present a complex and considerable challenge for all concerned – GPs, nurses, social workers, spiritual advisers and pharmacists. In learning to provide effective care, they will themselves usually have to face aspects of the same experience. Individual health professionals will need to come to terms with death and the process of dying, and to recognise the stress associated with being involved – even at a distance – with this special group of patients.

Sadly, at present, it is acknowledged that there is a gap between current practice and the optimum in palliative care. Patients can, and do, suffer from ineffectively controlled pain, cough, dyspnoea and insomnia. There is still a gulf between the problems perceived by the patient and those perceived by the doctor initiating or coordinating the care. The main problems identified with present day palliative care are deficiency in communication, understanding pain relief, inadequate control of pain, and poor psychological management of dying patients and their families.

A health care professional involved in palliative care needs a variety of skills and attitudes, and a framework of factual knowledge within which to work. The knowledge and skills required include:

- awareness and understanding of the psychological factors involved in a patient with an incurable disease;
- awareness of the meaning of loss, grief and bereavement;
- awareness of his or her own emotional responses when dealing with the dying;
- knowledge of the therapeutic options available for high levels of symptom control;
- possessing the necessary communication skills;
- understanding of the role of the multidisciplinary team.

Palliative care depends heavily on teamwork and good communications. It is a highly personalised form of care and requires both an ability to relate to other people and an adequate understanding of the ways in which different professions can contribute to the care of the whole individual.

Pharmacists are in a unique position to contribute to palliative care through the application of their expertise on medicines and through the use and extension of their counselling skills.

Appendix A (*see* page 101) contains further information on useful organisations, such as the Macmillan Nursing Service; and Appendix B (*see* page 109) contains a selection of key organisations providing help and advice to health care professionals, patients and their families.

Further reading

Cartwright, A., Hockey, L. & Anderson, J.L. 1973. *Life Before Death*. Routledge and Kegan Paul, London

Doyle, D. 1987. *Domiciliary Terminal Care*. Churchill Livingstone, Edinburgh

1992 Directory of Hospice Services in the UK and the Republic of Ireland. St Christopher's Hospice Information Service, London

Griffin, J. 1991. *Dying With Dignity*. Office of Health Economics, London

Hull, R., Ellis, M. & Sargent, V. 1989. *Teamwork in Palliative Care*. Radcliffe
    Medical Press, Oxford
Johnson, I.S. *et al*. 1990. *What Do Hospices Do*? A survey of hospices in the UK
    and Republic of Ireland. *Br Med J* **300**: 791–3
Saunders, C. (Ed) 1990. *Hospice and Palliative Care*. Edward Arnold, London
Spilling, R. 1986. *Terminal Care at Home*. Oxford University Press, Oxford
Wilkes, E., Professor (Chairman) 1980. *Terminal Care*. *Report of a Working Group*
    Standing Medical Advisory Committee HMSO, London

2 Philosophy of Terminal Illness

James Hanratty

Acceptance of the reality of death

The prospect of the finality of death fills most people with apprehension or fear. Although many patients are aware of the nature of their illness, not all are prepared to talk about death. This reluctance must be respected by the carers whilst giving the patient every opportunity to discuss the subject. If patients can be encouraged to talk about the reality of death and to express their fears, much of their tension and anxiety may be alleviated.

It is never easy to determine exactly when to discontinue efforts to cure, and each case poses unique problems. These decisions require consultation with the family, medical and nursing colleagues and, if possible, with the patient; often it is the patient who will decide. Once a diagnosis has been confirmed and death is inevitable, a change of role and attitude is then required in the management of the illness by all those caring for the patient. There is nothing more to be done to *cure* the patient but there is an enormous amount to be done to *care* for the patient and to ensure that the remaining few weeks, or months, are spent in comfort and are free from mental and physical suffering. The process of dying requires devoted and skilful medical and nursing care.

Palliative care

Compassion for patients needs to be supplemented by practical intervention to provide relief from their distress. Such intervention needs to be given with competence, and this requires some expertise and knowledge of what is available and appropriate, as well as the capability to apply it efficiently. Close cooperation between doctors, nurses, pharmacists and other health care staff is therefore essential for effective delivery of palliative care.

Effective care of the 'terminal' patient requires compassion, competence and constant attention to detail, with every aspect of the patient's condition being considered.

Symptoms causing distress need to be identified, even anticipated, then relieved by effective therapy. The threshold at which these symptoms, especially pain, causes distress varies widely. It is personal to each individual and the social, cultural, religious and ethnic background of the patient play a part. It may, however, fluctuate from day-to-day being affected by the patient's general level of comfort, degree of anxiety or feelings of isolation. Patients can benefit from leisure activities compatible with their condition and interests.

The patient's wishes about treatment should be respected, and any therapy undertaken should be explained beforehand.

Box 2.1: Symptoms requiring attention in terminal illness

- Pain
- Dysphagia
- Sore mouth
- Micturition problems
- Fistulae
- Itching
- Weakness
- Oedema
- Cough
- Confusion
- Nausea and vomiting
- Thirst
- Constipation
- Bleeding
- Pressure sores

- Fungating lesions
- Immobility
- Ascites
- Hiccough
- Insomnia
- Anorexia
- Dry mouth
- Diarrhoea
- Discharge
- Skin trouble
- Smell
- Paralysis
- Dyspnoea
- Emotional problems
- Disfigurement

As the patient's vital functions begin to disintegrate there is a constant change of symptoms, many of which may be anticipated by a knowledge of the pathological state of the patient. Therapy needs to be flexible and reviewed constantly. Possible symptoms are set out in Box 2.1. It is easy to assume that every symptom causing distress is from the malignant disease, whereas discomfort may arise from other conditions such as dyspepsia, haemorrhoids, arthritis or neuralgia, and these should be relieved by appropriate specific treatment.

Whatever therapy is involved in palliative care of the patient, the following questions should be considered:

- Is this treatment really necessary for this patient at this time, i.e. is its purpose to give comfort and control distressing symptoms?
- Has the treatment any undesirable side effects or complications? If so, can these be anticipated or minimised?
- Is the treatment of sufficient importance to warrant a full explanation of its implications to the patient and/or relatives, giving them an opportunity to express an opinion with the option to accept or reject the treatment?

Communication in terminal illness

It is essential to keep the lines of communication open between the patient, doctor, other health care staff and relatives. This can be achieved in part by regular staff meetings, where discussion about patients and families who are posing problems can take place. Sometimes there may be concern about a patient who has particular needs or about relatives who are showing signs of strain and are in need of special support. The relevance of some therapeutic procedures may also need discussion.

Communication with a dying patient is not easy. It can be full of emotional hazards and very time consuming. It is not surprising therefore that it is often avoided. There are three guidelines in talking to patients:

1   Always be truthful.
2   Patients, if they ask, have an absolute right to be told whatever they wish to know about their diagnosis and prognosis.
3   Equally, patients have a right *not* to have information which they are *not* seeking thrust upon them. Therefore patients should be given ample opportunity to signify their wishes.

It is impossible to soften the impact of bad news. However, it is important to let the patient determine the pace of the discussion. Perception of the implications takes time and the patient's response may be very slow. Allowances should be made for this during the consultation.

A patient's expectations are relative to his/her circumstances. The big hope is for a complete cure and restoration to normal good health. Such hope is unrealistic and the patient knows this. There are, however, many little hopes and these can achieve great importance in the patient's day to day life.

The protectiveness of relatives is understandable and may extend to their desire to shield the patient from all knowledge of the diagnosis and prognosis. Relatives should be reassured that any discussion with the patient will be conducted in a gentle and supportive manner, and that they will be kept fully informed.

The reactions and fears of the dying patient

Once a patient realises that death is approaching, it is essential to give ample time and opportunity for discussing the implications of this realisation. The patient may wish to have contact with a spiritual adviser. Even if religious interests have lapsed, a renewal at this time can bring comfort and peace. A legal adviser may also be necessary, and a social worker can help with domestic affairs.

Complete insight does not necessarily imply complete acceptance. Some patients do accept the knowledge of their impending death with quiet resignation and complete placidity. Others, however, may have a kaleidoscope of changing emotions.

Increased interest in people's mental and emotional reactions is important in palliative care, and there should be concern for total physical, mental, emotional, spiritual and social needs. Pharmacists need to be aware of the psychological aspects of terminal illness. The current understanding of dying owes much to the work of Dr Elisabeth Kubler-Ross, an American psychologist, who depicted terminal illness as an event occurring in five stages:

- denial and isolation;
- anger;
- bargaining;
- depression;
- acceptance.

She emphasised that throughout these stages hope always persists. The model is useful in signposting important psychological states that commonly occur as well as their likely sequence.

Denial acts as a buffer and allows a person time to collect him or herself and mobilise other defences. It is usually a temporary defence and is soon replaced by partial acceptance.

Isolation, in the form of social isolation, is a common problem for the terminally ill. In part, loss of energy and physical distress are the causative factors.

Anger can occur, although patients are more likely to admit to feeling bitter rather than angry. Typically, the patient is one who responded well to early treatment for cancer and then suddenly finds he or she is dying from extensive metastases. When anger is present, there is a need to accept and encourage its expression; once the emotional storm has passed, the patient will feel better and the situation will be easier to handle.

Bargaining is a method patients use to postpone death. It is a mental, often secret contract, which enables them to achieve a short-term aim. Patients with insight sometimes use the method to add purpose to life; small goals are set and usually achieved.

Depression can occur at any stage of life and its presence in the dying is not surprising. The depression can encompass a reaction to losses that have occurred already and anticipation of impending losses. There is a belief that the latter form of 'preparatory depression' is necessary and beneficial if the patient is to die in a state of acceptance and peace.

Acceptance is a stage almost void of feeling; a time of final rest. Patients often wish to be left alone and not disturbed by news and problems of the outside world. Patients in this state are without fear or despair.

Anxiety is experienced by most people when confronted by the unknown. This applies to approaching death although fear of death itself is perhaps less common than expected. This is especially so in older people, who may have lost a spouse or loved relative and are sustained in their dying by an anticipation of reunion with the loved person. Anxiety, when present, tends to be centred more on the process of dying than on death itself. Common fears are of pain, incontinence, dementia, of choking to death and of dying alone. The fears may be real or imaginery but they need to be expressed and discussed. The level of information given is that desired by the patient at the time, with most patients wishing to be fully informed. A key issue is how best to share the information.

'Separation anxiety' is the most common fear experienced by patients with terminal cancer. The patient is concerned about losses and the disruption of important relationships established during life. If the threat of death causes an upsurge of separation anxiety, then the presence of a close relative does more to bring peace to a dying person than any other measure.

Home care

If asked where they would prefer to be for their final illness most people would opt for their own home, provided that essential care would be available. Fifty years ago most patients (about two thirds) did remain at home for their final illness. Now it is the converse.

When it is apparent that a patient is nearing the terminal stage of a progressive, incurable illness, a meeting of all interested parties should be held including the patient, family, doctor and nurse, to discuss future management and plans. Certain questions require answers.

- What are the patient's wishes?
- What are the carers' wishes?
- Is the home suitable?
- Are there the necessary amenities, e.g. heating, bath, lavatory, and are these conveniently accessible?
- Should the patient be moved to another room?
- Who is available to provide the care at home and are they willing, available and capable?
- Are there good communications such as a telephone? Otherwise, what are the plans for obtaining assistance?
- Secure the help of community services, including the pharmacist.
- Are the general practitioner and nursing services able to carry the burden of frequent and sometimes lengthy visits?
- What other support, e.g. Macmillan nurses or hospice home care services, are available?
- Make advance plans on what to do should home care support break down, or patient and/or carers change their minds and prefer inpatient care.
- Is there an adjacent hospice? In any case contact the nearest hospice to obtain advice on specific problems.

Perhaps the most important aspect of home care is continuity of care by the same team. Emergency visits from total strangers are a poor substitute.

The carers and patient should understand clearly what medication is being given and what it is for. A chart listing all medication with times of dosage should be left in the house. The pharmacist's help should be sought on all aspects of medication, for example, continuity of supply. Medical and/or nursing notes left in the house should be simple and clear so that someone unfamiliar with the patient will be able to provide appropriate treatment.

Caring for the carers

The carer at home is often a woman – a mother, daughter, or in-law, and occasionally no relation at all. The professional carers, however devoted, are just short-term visitors to the home, and the continuing strain of coping with a seriously ill person inevitably rests with the resident carer, often with no respite. The effect of the unrelenting responsibility will soon lead to various forms of tension. The carer will feel isolated, unable to enjoy normal social activities and have a diminished quality of life.

Appropriate support is therefore essential right from the beginning; for example:

- reassurance that someone will always be available should anxieties arise;
- volunteer support from the local community, for example church, neighbours. Support from the local pharmacist, usually of a practical nature, is often crucial;
- arranging a night sitter, Marie Curie nurse, Meals on Wheels, laundry service;
- periodic attendance at a day centre if there is one available and if the patient's condition permits;
- respite admissions to local hospice or hospital;
- ensuring that all statutory supplementary payments are being received;
- trying to arrange that professional care is given by the same people.

Ethical issues in terminal illness

Communication

It cannot be over-emphasised that open and honest communication on all sides is paramount in achieving trust in terminal care. The relationship between the caring team, patient and family is based on trust, it is fostered by friendliness and it is destroyed by deceit or suspicion; and once destroyed it can never be regained.

Prognosis is an inexact art. Assessments in terms of days, weeks or months should be avoided. It is unacceptable to tailor the prognosis in over-optimistic terms to suit and please the patient, while giving a completely different prognosis to others.

Refusal of treatment

It is a patient's right to accept or refuse treatment. It is, however, essential that the patient should realise the implications so that an informed decision can be made. A full, detailed and impartial explanation should be given; ample time for discussion and, if necessary, further professional opinions should be made available. The pharmacist can be helpful here.

Some patients understandably reject chemotherapy or surgery for fear of unpleasant complications. The pros and cons should be set out clearly. A refusal is easier to accept if it is treatment which is unlikely to produce a cure, or will just provide temporary amelioration at the expense of much discomfort. Patients, because of their illness, are essentially vulnerable and should not be pressurised to make a decision which conflicts with their inclinations. However, it can be hard for carers when a patient refuses treatment which will certainly give comfort and relieve distress, for example, a patient who refuses to have morphine for severe pain. Nevertheless, such a refusal must be accepted if that is the patient's firm and informed decision. The acceptance by the carers of such a decision must be complete and the patient must not be treated with discourtesy for going against the carer's or professional staff's advice.

Refusal of treatment may be by a patient who is mentally confused or paranoid. Here, persuasion may be used and often succeeds. It is quite wrong to disguise drugs and give them surreptitiously, such as in their food or drink. If, however, a patient has a florid psychosis where sedation is vital, it is then justifiable to administer a drug against the patient's wishes, as it is for the patient's own safety.

Fringe or unorthodox treatment

Some patients who have not responded to orthodox medicine may seek treatment from unorthodox sources. Such treatment may be offensive to the patient's doctors but, provided it is offered and given in good faith and is unlikely to do any harm, for example certain types of diet or exercises, it must be accepted.

There are, however, 'fringe' treatments promoted purely for monetary gain from vulnerable people. Patients and families should be dissuaded in very strong terms from participating in these so-called treatments.

Euthanasia

No-one concerned with the delivery of palliative care can ignore the debate over euthanasia. All care-givers need to be sure who (dying patient or distressed onlooker) is expressing the wish for euthanasia and also to distinguish between statements like: 'I want to die', 'Allow me to die' and 'Kill me'. These should be regarded as cries for help.

Euthanasia is sometimes thought of as an insurance against a time when 'the pain becomes too bad'. In practice, it is common for patients who have talked of suicide to have the necessary drugs available but, perhaps for that very reason, not to feel the need to take them.

The following points are important.

1.   Skilful palliative care *is* becoming widely available. Pain and other distressing symptoms can almost always be controlled – with the patient remaining alert and in control.
2.   For a small number of patients controlling symptoms may necessitate increasing medication to high levels. But even if such carefully considered prescribing does appear to shorten life this is *not* euthanasia, it is good and careful medicine.

3. The artificial prolonging of life (dreaded by so many) involves a different debate. Calling a halt to inappropriate treatment is *not* euthanasia.
4. Euthanasia, an active intervention to end life, must never be included in the concept of palliative or hospice care. It would soon become the easy option and would undermine all that has been strived for and achieved to date. It would most certainly destroy all trust and progress.
5. Good medicine *is* needed. Bad law is not.

Ethical problems in ethnic groups

Language difficulties pose many problems especially if the patient and family come from an ethnic group with its own language. It is absolutely essential that effective interpretation be achieved so that the patient and the family are fully cognisant of the patient's illness, prognosis and treatment being given, and also are able to ask questions and express anxieties and fears.

Cultural attitudes may cause problems. For example, there are some ethnic groups where women are not allowed to express any opinions for themselves and the men regard it as their duty to monitor every aspect of care, including medical and nursing procedures. This attitude sometimes arouses antagonism in staff providing the care.

It is helpful to be aware of the religious and cultural attitudes of various ethnic groups with regard to the practices adopted when the patient dies and also with the procedures for the care of the body and its disposal. A most helpful text on this subject, *Caring for Dying People of Different Faiths* (1989. Lisa Sainsbury Foundation Series, Austen Cornish Publishers) has been written by Rabbi Julia Neuberger.

Physiology of dying

The five vital systems of the body – the cardiovascular, pulmonary, gastrointestinal, renal and central nervous systems have complex, mutually supportive interactions and if one system breaks down there is a knock-on effect on the other systems. As the deficiencies multiply a constantly changing kaleidoscope of symptoms develops. At this stage the main concern is to ensure, by palliative care, that none of these symptoms cause distress.

Causes of death

Once a patient has entered the terminal phase, it must be accepted that sudden death is always a possibility. Relatives should be forewarned

accordingly and at the same time given a full but simplified explanation
of the patient's illness.

There may be a sudden internal or external haemorrhage due to
tumour erosion of a major blood vessel, a massive embolus affecting the
lungs or brain, or acute heart failure or acute pulmonary oedema. It is,
however, more usual for the patient to move gradually towards the
closing stages of life by the progressive dysfunction of one or more of
the major systems.

The cardiovascular system

Abnormalities within the heart itself, for example coronary disease, may
cause arrhythmias. There may be diminution of circulatory volume as in
shock or haemorrhage. A breakdown of the other systems will also
affect heart action, for example electrolytic disturbances or severe
anaemia. The resultant defective pumping action of the heart in turn
leads to hypoxia elsewhere.

Major resuscitative procedures are irrelevant for the heart failure
supervening in terminal illness. Efforts should be concentrated on
controlling whatever symptoms arise that are distressing to the patient.

The pulmonary system

Defective oxygenation from pulmonary dysfunction may arise from:
infection; tumour infiltration; bronchospasm or asthma; oedema;
effusion; pneumothorax or infarct. Specific symptomatic treatment
should provide considerable relief from any distress occasioned by these
conditions, but cerebral hypoxia may develop. A common cause of
death is infection leading to pneumonia.

The gastrointestinal and renal systems

Obstructions, infections, tumour infiltration and liver or renal failure
may cause various toxic and electrolytic disturbances affecting heart and
brain function. Uraemia, in particular, is common.

The central nervous system

The brain and spinal cord are particularly vulnerable to any condition
occupying extra space or causing increased pressure. The factors which
can damage the central nervous system are: infections, for example
meningitis, encephalitis, brain abscess; blood vessel disruption or
obstruction, for example thrombosis, haemorrhage, emboli; toxic and
metabolic disorders, for example from renal or liver failure or extraneous
poisons such as drugs; malignant tumours – primary or metastatic – and

hypoxia due to circulatory or pulmonary failure. Hypoxia and defective blood circulation in the brain lead to the accumulation of toxic metabolites such as lactic acid. This is a major cause of brain death as the process initiates swelling which raises intracranial pressure and further reduces the circulation and oxygen supply.

The signs of central nervous system dysfunction are, in progression: confusion and disorientation; lethargy and apathy; stupor; semi-coma and coma. The deterioration is usually uneven and there are often marked fluctuations from one state to another.

As brain hypoxia worsens the pupils dilate and eventually become unresponsive to light. The blood pressure falls and the pulse becomes rapid, feeble and irregular. Occasionally convulsive seizures may occur. Cheyne-Stokes breathing is very common with cerebral hypoxia and the rapid breathing is interrupted by periods of apnoea which become more and more prolonged.

While it is unlikely that community pharmacists will be directly involved at the death of a patient, the following paragraphs provide valuable background information.

Approaching death

Impairment of consciousness in the form of stupor and coma becomes the norm as death approaches. Few people pass from life to death in a state of clear consciousness; only 12% of patients are fully alert 24 hours before death, while 30–40% are already comatose.

Patients at this stage should not be left alone. Someone sitting quietly holding the patient's hand will give great comfort and support. Family or friends are usually in attendance and they should be kept fully informed about what is happening; for instance, changing patterns of breathing and the nature and purpose of any treatment being given.

Restlessness may be due to the withdrawal reactions of the patient's medication when opioids have been suddenly discontinued perhaps because the patient can no longer swallow. If the patient cannot take the medication orally it should be given by injection.

Faecal impaction should not have been allowed to develop but it may be a cause of much discomfort. Urinary retention is a common cause of restlessness and may easily be overlooked – catheterisation will be necessary. Lying in an awkward position or on a pressure sore will obviously cause discomfort. Extreme dryness of the mouth or eyes is also uncomfortable. Moisturising with methylcellulose applications is very soothing.

Noisy breathing (the death rattle) is due to secretions in the trachea and larynx which the patient is unable to cough up. If copious, suction will help and the patient should be placed well on to one side so that the

secretions can drain away. A sub-cutaneous injection of hyoscine 0.4 mg
may also be helpful, or if there is pulmonary oedema, frusemide may be
necessary. If the patient continues to be restless, useful parenteral
agents to help relaxation are Nozinan (methotrimeprazine) 25 mg,
Largactil (chlorpromazine) 50 mg or Ativan (lorazepam) 2 mg to 4 mg.

Signs of death

Signs of death are the absence of pulse and respiration, confirmed by the
absence of auscultatory sounds over the heart and trachea for at least
five minutes. The pupils are fixed and dilated, and the fundi oculi show
fragmentation of blood in the retinal veins.

Further reading

Hanratty, J.F. 1989. *Palliative Care of the Terminally Ill*. Radcliffe Medical Press,
    Oxford
Kubler-Ross, E. 1970. *On Death and Dying*. Tavistock Publications, London
Neuberger, J. 1989. *Caring for Dying People of Different Faiths*. The Lisa Sainsbury
    Foundation Series, Austen Cornish Publishers
Stedeford, A. 1984. *Facing Death. Patients, Families and Professionals*. William
    Heinemann, London
Twycross, R.G. 1982. *The Dying Patient*. Christian Medical Fellowship
    Publication, London

3 Palliative Care

Tom West

Much of our experience in controlling the suffering of those who are terminally ill is based on the hospice experience of caring for patients with advanced cancer. However, the principles underlying good symptom control can also be applied in the management of non-malignant conditions such as motor neurone disease or AIDS. Effective symptom control remains the cornerstone of palliative care. Good symptom control should be practised throughout the course of any disease and should not be withheld because active treatment is still under way. This applies, for example, to vomiting, a common side-effect of radiotherapy. The symptom is unacceptable for the patient and should be controlled through the use of an appropriate antiemetic.

Most of the patients requiring terminal care will have progressed from active treatment and often there is an overlap between the two phases of care (*see* Fig. 3.1). The grey area, the place of decision, is all too often a time when no decisions are taken. But the arrows go in both directions and some patients, labelled terminal, may still benefit from further active treatment. The line between appropriate treatment on the one hand and inappropriate treatment on the other is often very fine.

The essential components of palliative care are:

- good symptom control; *which will allow*
- improved communication; *in turn leading to*
- relevant family support; which can be physical and psychological.

Patients with advanced cancer have many potential and varied problems, such that no one person has the expertise to deal with them all. A multidisciplinary approach is often required.

Symptom control

The symptoms listed in Box 3.1 are those refractory symptoms which can result in patients being admitted to a hospice. However, in many cases GPs are able to manage successfully a range of symptoms experienced by their patients. We shall discuss five of them, along with depression and confusion.

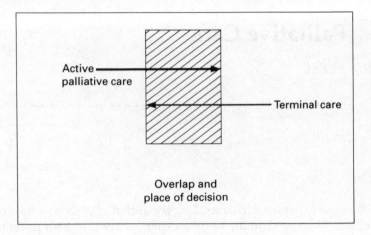

Figure 3.1　Overlap of the 'cure' and 'care' systems

Addressing such symptoms diligently and skilfully could prevent patients and their families so often reporting 'The doctor said nothing more could be done'. Indeed, unless distressing physical symptoms can be adequately dealt with, good terminal care is impossible. Asking the right questions at the outset and taking a detailed patient history are fundamental to making an accurate patient assessment. How effectively this is done determines how good the subsequent treatment will be. The initial assessment should be used as a base line for comparison with further assessment, measurements and observations. Once a thorough patient history has been taken, five key steps should be followed if symptoms are to be controlled effectively:

1　*Analyse the cause* It is important to compare the medical history with the patient's own idea of what caused the problem. Examination of the patient will provide further information to help reveal underlying pathology. For example, bone pain can arise from invasion of bone either by primary or metastatic tumours. The pain may be the presenting complaint, for example, in patients with carcinoma of the breast with secondary spread.

　　Potential causes of nausea and vomiting, a commonly occurring symptom, include hypercalcaemia, constipation, pain and fear. Emotional factors should always be considered.

　　Possible biochemical changes experienced by the patient, for example hypercalcaemia, may be the cause of the symptom, for example in nausea or vomiting. These changes are often reversible and warrant investigation.

Box 3.1: Common symptoms in patients on admission to St Christopher's Hospice	
Symptoms	**Patients affected (%)**
Weakness	92
Cachexia/weight loss	83
Anorexia	75
Pain	69
Dyspnoea	50
Nausea and vomiting	49
Constipation	48
Cough	47
Oedema/ascites/effusion	43
Insomnia	29

2 *Choose appropriate treatment* Having analysed the cause(s) of the symptom, a decision can be made on the appropriate treatment. As well as drugs, the doctor may have to consider surgery or radiotherapy (and for pain control, nerve blocks). Specialists in these fields, who understand the application of their skills in terminal care, can give valuable second opinions.

3 *Prescribe appropriately* Unless the drugs being prescribed are understood, they will not be used effectively. Six factors need to be considered:

- **site of action** e.g. NSAIDs used to reduce the production of tissue-sensitising prostaglandins, for instance in bone pain;
- **duration of action** e.g. MST 12 hourly: pethidine 2–3 hourly;
- **dosage range** e.g. normal dose range often extended e.g. in the use of laxatives, co-danthramer 10–30 ml bd;
- **symptom response** e.g. antidepressants: up to 14 days; when used as a co-analgesic, more rapid response achieved;
- **side effects** e.g. opioids: constipation;
- **interactions** e.g. dexamethasone and phenytoin; concomitant administration results in reduced effect of the corticosteroid.

Clearly it is wise for prescribers to use a limited number of drugs and to become familiar with their therapeutic actions and associated problems.

Drug regimens should be made as simple as possible and polypharmacy kept to a minimum in order to maximise compliance. One aim should be for a drug suitable to be given on a twice daily basis, e.g. a pharmacist could help in the choice of an appropriate NSAID. Whenever possible, drugs should be given by the oral route which is flexible and maintains the patient's independence. If swallowing becomes difficult the use of the sublingual or rectal routes should be considered. Although some patients may prefer a small volume injection to a suppository, the parenteral route is usually more hazardous, inconvenient and unpleasant and should normally only be necessary in the last few days or hours of life.

4   *Psychosocial and spiritual factors* Good manners together with competence can give a much needed sense of security. Improved communication will lead to family involvement and support. An acknowledgement of a spiritual dimension to living and dying can help with feelings of guilt, anger, fear and meaninglessness.

5   *Review* A review of the patient and of all medication must be carried out regularly and frequently. Treatment must be acceptable as well as effective. Treatment must always be adapted to the patient's changing circumstances and may involve:

- adjustment of the prescribed dose
- withdrawal of a drug
- addition of another drug
- substitution of one drug by another in the same group.

For example, a patient's taste buds can change during the course of a terminal illness by becoming intolerant to the sweet taste of lactulose. This factor can dictate the choice of laxative as taste or volume of solution will have to be considered as well as its pharmacological action.

Pharmacists are in a position to encourage families and patients to ask for better symptom control. The prescriber will achieve this through the most appropriate use of drugs (given the prevailing circumstances) and regular review.

Pain

Pain is probably the symptom most dreaded by patients with a life-threatening disease. In such patients there may well be

- physical
- mental
- social and
- spiritual

components, needing to be identified, evaluated and treated. In this process it is important not to lose sight of all these aspects in relation to the patient's well being. Figure 3.2 provides a diagrammatic representation of the components of total pain.

Pain is a complex subjective experience which has a cognitive and an affective component. The cognitive component is the actual perception of the painful stimuli and the affective component is the variable emotional response of an individual to those particular stimuli. *Pain threshold* is the intensity of stimulation at which pain is first perceived and is a relatively constant quantity which differs little between

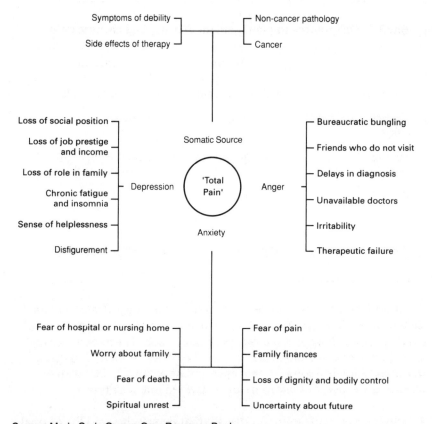

Source: Marie Curie Cancer Care Resource Book

Figure 3.2 Diagrammatic representation of the components of total pain

individuals. *Pain tolerance* varies enormously from person to person and also within the same individual at different times under different circumstances. Many things lower pain tolerance and successful analgesia often requires more than the administration of analgesics. Many of the factors illustrated in Fig. 3.2 will require identification and relief. This, together with the use of conventional analgesics and/or physical methods, such as neurolytic blocks or radiotherapy, can bring about effective pain relief.

Physical pain

Most of us are far more familiar with the symptoms of acute pain, for example post-operative pain than we are with those of chronic pain, for example in arthritis and terminal cancer. The management of these conditions differs markedly, as illustrated in Box 3.2.

Box 3.2 Differences in management of acute and chronic pain		
	Acute	**Chronic**
Sedation	Often desirable	Usually undesirable
Desired duration of effect	2–4 hours	Continuous
Timing of analgesic	As required	Regular dosing to pre-empt pain breakthrough
Dose	Within a narrow range (as seen in BNF)	Individually determined; wide range of doses
Route	Injection	By mouth, suppository or syringe driver

Acute and chronic pain are very different and distinct. *Acute pain* can be defined as pain which results from an acute injury or disease state and persists only as long as the tissue pathology itself. The experience of acute pain serves a biological function; the patient is alerted to the fact that something is wrong, so that appropriate action can be taken to remove the cause. *Chronic pain* can be divided into four types:

- pain from an acute injury or disease that persists beyond the normal healing time

- pain related to a chronic degenerative disease or persisting neurological condition
- pain that emerges without an identifiable organic cause and persists episodically
- pain associated with advanced malignant disease

Chronic pain has lost its diagnostic value and serves no biological function. Psychological factors are extremely important in the development of chronic pain. Cancer pain is often described as chronic and increasing over time. It can result from tumour infiltration of:

- bone
- nerves
- viscera, or
- soft tissue.

Pain caused by these mechanisms may need to be treated in different ways. If pain relief is to be effective it is essential that the mechanism underlying the pain is identified, then appropriate treatment can be started.

Analgesia

The major goal of chronic pain management is to maintain continuous control of pain, whilst allowing the patient to remain alert. Analgesics are administered on a regular basis, according to their known duration of action, so that pain does not break through before the next dose is given. 'See if you can do a little longer without the pain killer' is the worst possible prescription for good pain control. There is no standard or maximum dose for pain control and doses are determined on an individual basis. The minimum effective dose will vary greatly between patients. The right dose of an analgesic is that which gives relief for the whole of the dosage interval, which should be a minimum of four hours.

Analysing the cause of pain is extremely important. Different causes of pain require different approaches. Most patients experience more than one type of pain, often at different sites and with different aetiology. Before starting treatment, it is essential that an accurate record of the location and quality of the pain is obtained. This will help to establish the underlying cause of the pain and will also act as a baseline in assessing the efficacy of the various pain-relieving strategies used. Body charts are usefully employed in this situation. A typical chart and a description of how it is completed is provided in Appendix C.

An assessment of the nature and degree of the patient's pain stems from a careful history, from observation and examination and from a knowledge of the patient's drug history. In establishing the latter, the following should be noted for each drug:

- actual amount taken, rather than amount prescribed
- effect on the individual pain
- side effects experienced.

Careful evaluation of all the information should result in an initial pain assessment. A reasonable choice of analgesic can then be made. It is not uncommon for a patient to require more than one modality of treatment.

Box 3.3 A basic analgesic ladder

Category	Parent drug	Alternatives
Strong opioid	morphine	diamorphine morphine sulphate continus (MST) phenazocine (Narphen)
Weak opioid	codeine	dextropropoxyphene (e.g. in Co-proxamol) dihydrocodeine oxycodone pectinate (Proladone suppository)
Non-opioid	aspirin	paracetamol flurbiprofen (Froben) naproxen (e.g. Naprosyn)

The three basic analgesics are aspirin, codeine and morphine. There are some basic rules for their use and for the use of alternative analgesics:

- in general, if a drug fails to relieve the pain move up – not across – the ladder;
- aspirin, flurbiprofen or naproxen will relieve bone pain better than the opioids – in these cases moving across the ladder can be advantageous;
- pethidine and dextromoramide (Palfium) are so short-acting that they have no role as principal analgesics in terminal care; and
- it is best to avoid using an agonist-antagonist* e.g. pentazocine

*Agonist – a drug which combines with a receptor, activates it and initiates a sequence of events; antagonists – a drug which interferes with the action of an agonist.

(Fortral) of a partial agonist e.g. buprenorphine (Temgesic) – their role in the treatment of cancer pain is debatable due to their associated side effects.

Pharmacological properties of opioid analgesics and antagonists

The term 'opioid' is used to describe a group of drugs that are morphine-like in their properties. Opioids interact with what appear to be closely related receptors, and they share some of the properties of certain naturally-occurring peptides – the enkephalins, the endorphins and the dynorphins. Each is derived from a distinct precursor polypeptide and has a characteristic anatomical distribution.

The word opioid refers in a generic sense to all drugs, natural and synthetic, with morphine-like actions. The term 'narcotic' is considered no longer useful in a pharmacological context.

Multiple opioid receptors

A number of opioid receptor types exist at specific sites in the brain and other organs. There is reasonably firm evidence for three major categories of receptors, which are designated μ (mu), κ (kappa), δ (delta). Opioids are generally classified into three groups:

- morphine-like opioid agonists – substances acting as agonists primarily at μ, κ and perhaps δ receptors
- opioid antagonists – substances such as naxolone that are devoid of agonist activity at any receptor
- opioid with mixed actions, which includes agonist-antagonists (e.g. pentazocine) and the partial agonists (e.g. buprenorphine)

There are many compounds that produce analgesia and other effects similar to those produced by morphine. Morphine remains the standard against which new analgesics are assessed.

Central nervous system (CNS)

Morphine-like drugs produce analgesia, drowsiness, changes in mood and mental cloudiness. When therapeutic doses of morphine are given to patients with pain, they report that they are aware of the pain but that they are much less bothered by it. All types of painful experiences include both the original sensation and the reaction to that sensation. Opioids blunt the response to painful stimuli at several loci in the CNS. The sensation of pain is altered by opioid analgesics and the affective response is also changed. A patient's ability to tolerate the pain may be markedly increased even when the capacity to perceive the sensation is relatively unaltered.

Non-steroidal anti-inflammatory drugs (NSAIDs)

NSAIDs are potent inhibitors of prostaglandin synthetase. Their precise mode of action is complex. Although they exert their main pain-relieving action at peripheral sites, it appears that there is a central component to their analgesic action.

The drugs in Box 3.4 have been found most acceptable in terms of efficacy and patient compliance. Analgesics such as aspirin and paracetamol should not be underestimated as they are highly effective in some patients. The usual precautions in the use of NSAIDs apply equally in terminal situations.

Mental pain

Sadness and depression are often hard to distinguish. Sadness has been described as being *filled up* with feelings, while depression can be thought of as being *emptied* of feelings. Sadness may well be appropriate and therefore needs acknowledging and sharing. Depression is a common emotion in the terminal stages of an illness. It should be diagnosed positively and the attendant insomnia could be treated if required. (See section on Depression, page 32.) Fear can be a powerful factor in mental pain, and may arise from bad memories of other family deaths or a dread of the unknown future. Encouragement to recall bad times or to express such fears, followed by appropriate explanations and reassurance, can be helpful.

Social pain

Family responsibilities and stresses, and poor communication within a family are potent sources of pain. Gently exploring the family history and dynamics, dealing carefully with such statements as 'He mustn't be told, he'd give up if he knew', and suggesting that untapped and often considerable family strengths should be mobilised, can all help to turn a time of loss and bereavement into a time of mutual support and growth.

Box 3.4 Nonsteroidal analgesics			
Approved name/ Trade name	**Presentation**	**Typical dose**	**Comment**
Aspirin	Tablet: 300 mg	600 mg 4–6 hourly	Dyspepsia occurs in 25% of regular users. Increases methotrexate level. Enhances effect of oral anticoagulants.
Paracetamol	Tablet: 500 mg	1 g 4–6 hourly	Soluble tablet available. Caution in liver impairment.
Diflunisal (Dolobid)	Tablet: 250 mg 500 mg	500–750 mg every 12 hours	Well tolerated. Twice daily dose maximises compliance. Good first line agent. Caution in patients receiving anti-coagulants. Concurrent administration of aluminium based antacids with NSAIDs should be avoided. Caution in renal impairment.
Flurbiprofen (Froben)	Tablet: 50 mg 100 mg	100 mg every 12 hours	Well tolerated. First line agent. May cause diarrhoea in same patients.
Naproxen (Naprosyn, Synflex)	Tablet: 250 mg 500 mg Capsule: 275 mg (sodium salt)	500 mg every 12 hours	Well tolerated. First line agent.

Spiritual pain

Anger and guilt, a fist in the face of God, or the question 'Why should this happen to me . . .?' can seldom be dealt with by clever answers. A willingness to listen, to share and to stay alongside such pain, as well as a knowledge of where more professional help can be obtained (local ministers, leaders of different faiths, hospital chaplains) are useful. Often, what is really being asked for is our concern, rather than a quick referral on to a professional.

Further information on pain control is provided in Chapter 4.

Depression

Depression can often go undetected in patients with far-advanced disease. Patients may be slow to volunteer psychological symptoms and doctors may fail to ask about them. Depression in terminal illness is often, wrongly, regarded as 'appropriate' or 'untreatable'.

Symptoms which might alert one to the possibility of a patient being depressed include an inability to take pleasure in anything; a low mood; loss of concentration e.g. inability to read a newspaper; a disturbed sleep pattern; persistent tearfulness; irritability; and a sense of worthlessness.

Obviously, a previous psychiatric history should be asked about and, perhaps equally important, the patient's reactions and coping mechanism to previous traumatic life-events should be explored. Family and friends may usefully be consulted.

Possible reversible causes of psychiatric disturbance such as brain tumours, medication (e.g. steroids, opioids, the benzodiazepines and some chemotherapeutic agents), hypercalcaemia and, most importantly, severe uncontrolled pain, must all be considered. Psychosocial issues may also be exacerbating the situation.

Treatment. In the terminal stages of illness emotional support from family, friends, physicians, nurses and other professionals is the most important and valuable approach. It is often difficult to decide when to add antidepressants. Most antidepressants take ten days or more to exert their antidepressant effect, although patients may benefit from the anxiolytic or sedative effect much earlier. When antidepressants are prescribed pharmacists can encourage patients to persevere with their medication and should also be aware of possible side effects. These include a dry mouth, blurred vision, hesitancy of micturition and constipation. Elderly patients, in particular, should be warned of possible postural hypotension and be advised to 'get up in stages'.

Patients with advanced disease should always be started on a very low dose of antidepressant (e.g. amitriptyline 25 mg per day) and worked up gradually to a therapeutic dose, which may be lower than that needed in younger or healthier individuals. The choice of antidepressant should largely depend on the clinical state of the patient. Depressed patients with agitation, anxiety and insomnia would benefit from the sedative properties of such drugs as dothiepin, amitriptyline or trimipramine, while patients with diminished abilities and retarded mental function might respond better to a less sedative compound such as imipramine.

Depression is not an inevitable accompaniment of terminal illness. However, when symptoms are identified antidepressant medication combined with emotional support is likely to be more effective than emotional support alone. Pharmacists can help in picking up the signs of depression, in advising a more direct approach to the doctor ('Doctor, could I be depressed?'), in explaining side effects and in encouraging patients to persist with their treatment.

Nausea and vomiting

Nausea and vomiting are common symptoms in terminal disease and can be very distressing for both patient and family.

Vomiting starts with salivation and nausea and ends with the gastric contents being expelled. Vomiting, like breathing, is a somatic not autonomic process and therefore continues after interruption of all autonomic activity.

Nausea and vomiting result from stimulation of the chemoreceptor trigger zone and/or vomiting centre in the medulla oblongata. The vomiting centre is the final common pathway for the initiation of vomiting from any cause, co-ordinating input from the gastrointestinal

---

Box 3.5: Neurotransmitter receptors and their sites in the brain

Neurotransmitter receptor	Site
Dopamine (D_2)	Chemoreceptor trigger zone
Histamine (H_1)	Vomiting centre Vestibular centre
Muscarinic cholinergic	Vomiting centre Vestibular centre
Serotonin (5HT3)	Chemoreceptor trigger zone Nucleus tractus solitarius

tract via the vagus, cerebral cortex, hypothalmus, vestibular centre and chemoreceptor trigger zone (CTZ). The latter is sensitive to many drugs (including morphine and its derivatives) and to certain substances produced in the body by different disease states (*see* Fig. 3.3).

At least four different neurotransmitter receptors have been isolated in the areas of the brain which regulate vomiting, thus providing at least four possible mechanisms of action for antiemetic drugs.

Antiemetic drugs can therefore be classified according to their pharmacological group, site of action and effect on specific neurotransmitters.

As it is a protective reflex, vomiting is often a symptom of underlying pathology. This should be identified and appropriate specific therapy initiated. Antiemetics are a non-specific measure. The choice of agent depends on site of action, routes available and patient acceptability.

Box 3.6: Classification of antiemetic drugs

Pharmacological group	Putative site of action	Receptor affected
Anticholinergics e.g. atropine, hyoscine	Vomiting centre	Muscarinic cholinergic
Antihistamines e.g. cyclizine, diphenhydramine	Vomiting centre	Histamine (H_1)
Phenothiazines e.g. prochlorperazine, methotrimeprazine	Chemoreceptor trigger zone (low doses) Vomiting centre (high doses)	Dopamine (D_2) Histamine (H_1)
Butyrophenones e.g. haloperidol, droperidol	Chemoreceptor trigger zone	Dopamine (D_2)
Dopamine antagonists e.g. metoclopramide, domperidone	Chemoreceptor trigger zone	Dopamine (D_2)
Sedatives e.g. lorazepam	Chemoreceptor trigger zone	?
Selective serotonin-receptor antagonists	Chemoreceptor trigger zone nucleus tractus solitarius	Serotonin ($5HT_3$)

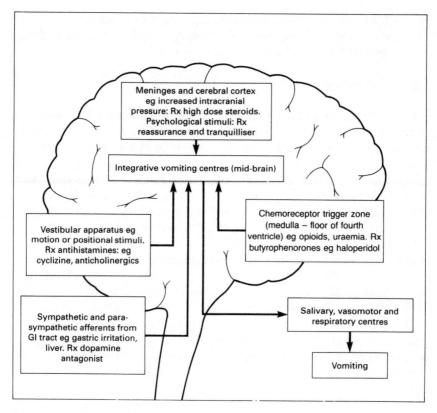

Adapted from: *Geriatric Medicine*. 1987. **28**, 63–66.

Figure 3.3 The vomiting mechanism

Occasionally it may be necessary to use up to three antiemetics with differing sites of action in order to control the symptoms. Where vomiting proves intractable, medication should be reduced to a minimum and be given by continuous SC/IV infusion, intermittent rectal or parenteral administration.

The causes of nausea and vomiting can be divided into four groups:

- *Iatrogenic*. Some drugs (e.g. the opioids) may act centrally; others (e.g. NSAIDs) may cause gastric irritation.
- *Organic*. Faecal impaction, a stomach 'squashed' by an enlarged liver or ascites, bowel obstruction or raised intra-cranial pressure need to be considered.
- *Metabolic*. Uraemia or hypercalcaemia may present with nausea or vomiting.
- *Psychological*. Anxiety or fear are potent exacerbaters of any physical symptom.

Reversible causes of nausea and vomiting should be treated. Consideration should be given to the presence of faecal impaction, drug effects, perhaps hypercalcaemia, and/or uraemia.

Choice of antiemetic

If a patient is vomiting, it is useless to prescribe medication by mouth. Until the symptoms are brought under control, it might be necessary to give the prescribed antiemetic by suppository or by injection (*see* Box 3.7).

If nausea or vomiting is not controlled, the choice of antiemetic should be critically reviewed. The antiemetic may need to be changed to one with a different site of action; a second antiemetic may be added; or the dose of the original antiemetic may need to be increased.

In patients with refractory vomiting, e.g. those with intestinal obstruction, antiemetics may need to be given as a continual subcutaneous infusion using an ambulatory pump such as the Graseby MS26. Antiemetics may often be given in combination with diamorphine via this route.

The role of the serotonin receptor antagonists ondansetron and granisetron, in the control of vomiting in advanced cancer is at present unclear. Further work is required. The current use of these agents is largely restricted to those patients who are receiving platinum-containing chemotherapy regimes.

Psychological factors

Anxious families may need repeated reassurance that three meals a day are no longer appropriate. Providing small helpings of acceptable food will probably ease the concern so often associated with nausea and vomiting. IV fluids and even drinking can be inappropriate. Meticulous mouth care and sips of iced water may be all that is required at this stage.

As with the treatment of all symptoms, the regime adopted must be subject to regular review.

Dyspnoea

Pain may be the most feared symptom but dyspnoea is in fact the most frightening. The causes of dyspnoea fall into four groups (*see* Fig. 3.4).

- *Mechanical factors*. This can be disease within the lung (tumour, pneumonia, previous lung disease) or impairment of mechanical function of the lung (lymphangitis carcinomatosis, pulmonary

Box 3.7: Recommended antiemetic drugs

Pharmacological Group	Drug	Presentation	Typical dose	Comments
Anticholinergics	Hyoscine	Tablet: 300 µg Injection: 400 µg/ml 600 µg/ml	By mouth o SC 300–600 µg as necessary up to four times daily	Do not use in patients with glaucoma, paralytic ileus or pyloric stenosis. May cause drowsiness, blurred vision, difficulty with micturition (rare at antiemetic doses)
Antihistamines	Cyclizine (Valoid)	Tablet: 50 mg Injection: 50 mg/ml	50 mg tds	Caution in patients with prostatic hypertrophy, glaucoma, side effects may include drowsiness, blurred vision and gastric upset
Phenothiazines	Prochlorperazine (Stemetil)	Tablet: 5 mg and 25 mg Syrup: 5 mg/5 ml Injection: 12.5 mg/ml 1 ml and 2 ml Suppositories: 5 mg and 25 mg	active vomiting: 20 mg stat and then 10 mg after 2 hrs. Prophylactic 5–10 mg twice or thrice daily. 12.5 mg IM every six hours 25 mg rectally as required	Caution in patients taking antiparkinsonion drugs. Side effects rare at antiemetric dosage
Butyrophenones	Haloperidol (Haldol, Serenace)	Capsules: 500 µg Tablet: 1.5 mg and 5 mg Elixir: 2 mg/ml, 10 mg/ml Injection: 5 mg/ml, 1 ml and 2 ml	Active vomiting 2.5 mg IM prophylactic 0.5 mg – 1.5 mg twice or thrice daily	Drug of choice for opioid induced vomiting. Discontinue after five days. Side effects rare at antiemetic dosage
Dopamine antagonists	Metoclopramide (Maxolon, Primperan)	Tablet: 10 mg Syrup: 5 mg/5 ml Injection: 5 mg/ml 2 ml	All routes 10 mg thrice daily	Extrapyramidal side effects and drowsiness and constipation. Central and peripheral antiemetic effect
	Domperidone (Motilium)	Tablet: 10 mg Suspension: 5 mg/5 ml Suppositories: 30 mg	20 mg every four to six hours. 60 mg rectally every four to eight hours	Poor oral bioavailability (approx. 20%). Does not cross the blood brain barrier therefore lower incidence of side effects in comparison with metoclopramide. Expensive; try metoclopramide first
Sedatives	Lorazepam (Ativan)	Tablet: 1 mg and 2.5 mg Injection: 4 mg/ml 1 ml	Up to 6 mg daily in two or three divided doses	May help where there is a large functional component in nausea and vomiting
Miscellaneous	Pyridoxine (Vitamin B_6)	Tablet: 10 mg and 50 mg	60–150 mg daily	Vitamin B_6 may be depleted in some radiotherapy patients.

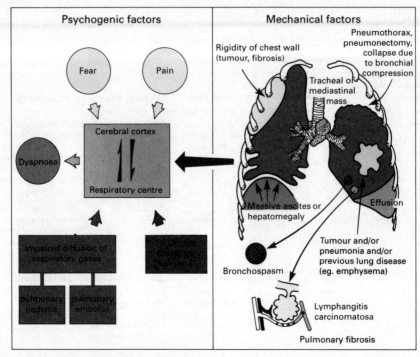

Source: Geriatric Medicine. 1987. **17**, 35–9.

Figure 3.4   Causes of dyspnoea (in malignant disease)

fibrosis, bronchospasm, collapse). It may also be disease outside the lung (pleural effusion, ascites or hepatomegaly, tracheal or mediastinal mass, rigidity of chest wall).

- *Impaired diffusion of respiratory gases*. Pulmonary oedema or pulmonary emboli.
- *Biochemical factors*. Anaemia or uraemia.
- *Psychogenic factors*. Fear of suffocating or choking; pain.

Treatment. There are five options for treating terminal malignant lung disease:

- Opioids. Correctly prescribed in small doses, regular morphine takes away the sensation of breathlessness.
- Tranquillisers. Are not used routinely as they can depress respiration. Diazepam probably has some specific action on the respiratory centre. Tranquillisers are used to treat the anxiety associated with dyspnoea.
- Hyoscine (scopolamine). This will help dry up excessive secretions. It will also help to control the 'death rattle'.
- Steroids. They may alleviate lymphangitis and mediastinal obstruction.
- Oxygen. Should be available, although in general the benefits are psychological rather than pharmalogical. Dyspnoea is usually managed in more appropriate ways.

Prescribe appropriately. If any nonmalignant cause of dyspnoea can be treated, this should be done. Opioids should be started with a low dose: morphine solution 5 mg four-hourly may well be adequate. It is unusual to need more than 10 to 20 mg four-hourly. Diazepam is prescribed 5 to 10 mg at night or 5 mg eight-hourly; hyoscine (Scopolamine) 0.4 to 0.6 mg four-hourly as required; dexamethasone (Decadron, Oradexon) 8 to 12 mg daily.

Constipation must not occur. Laxatives (e.g. Dioctyl and Senna) should be prescribed routinely with opioids. A rectal examination may be necessary.

Oral thrush must be treated, for example with nystatin (Nystan, Nystavescent suspension 1 to 2 ml every four hours).

Remember psychosocial factors. Feeling short of breath and the fear of suffocating can largely be subjective. Reassurance that the patient will not suffocate to death, appropriate diversion and a sense of security can be the most effective treatment. Suitable diversion may include getting the family to talk, distracting the patient to think of other things, and enabling patient, carers and staff to relax together.

Review, as ever, is essential.

Constipation

Many people believe that a daily bowel action is their rightful heritage. But as the end of life draws nearer a majority of patients will suffer from constipation. More anxiety can be provoked by this symptom than by any other and it needs to be taken seriously. An important first step is to ascertain the patient's normal bowel movement. A rectal examination is important for excluding the possibility of over flow diarrhoea.

The causes of constipation include inactivity, a diet low in roughage and the use of analgesic and other constipating drugs. Only too often, in patients with a terminal disease, these factors cannot be altered. But it may be worth suggesting that although bran may be unacceptable to the very ill, increasing the fluid intake is sometimes both acceptable and helpful.

The British National Formulary classifies laxatives into four main groups:

- bulk-forming drugs
- stimulant laxatives
- faecal softeners
- osmotic laxatives.

The classification disguises the fact that some laxatives have a complex action. Modes of action are described in the Formulary for each group of laxatives.

Pharmacists can help patients by explaining why constipation may have occurred; in reassuring patients and their families that a daily bowel action is not needed and in suggesting appropriate laxatives. Laxatives should be routinely prescribed whenever opioids are regularly prescribed. The latency and effect of all laxatives vary with dosage.

Treatment of faecal impaction, if it has been allowed to occur, must be dealt with. Bisacodyl (Dulcolax) and glycerine suppositories, or alternatively a phosphate enema, are often adequate but occasionally a manual removal or an oil-retention enema given at night may be necessary.

Most terminally ill patients are best managed with a combination of stool softener and stimulant laxatives. This will avoid either painful colic or a bowel loaded with soft faeces – problems which can arise if a stimulant or softening laxative is given alone. Co-danthramer (danthron and poloxamer) and co-danthrusate (danthron and dioctyl) are convenient, combined preparations. The dose should be gradually increased until a regular soft bowel action is obtained.

Occasionally, in spite of regular laxatives, the bowels do not open regularly and a good general rule is for a rectal examination to be performed on the third day, inserting suppositories if the rectum is loaded. This will avoid the physical and mental distress of patients who are constipated for a week or more.

A schematic approach to the treatment of constipation is reproduced in Fig. 3.5.

Confusion

Impairment of intellect is subtle and often overlooked. It can manifest itself as dementia or confusion and is common in the later stages of a terminal illness. The incidence of dementia amongst AIDS victims is high.

Confusion can be a most disturbing condition for a patient (and sometimes even more for a family) to face. The fear of 'going mad' and the need to explain 'that this is not really like him' call for understanding, explanation and support. Patients may be 'quietly muddled' as in Alzheimer's disease, or they may be agitated, disorientated and hallucinating as in the acute confusional state that may develop in a previously lucid cancer patient. In practice there is often a mixture of the two. An example is the elderly cancer patient with a mild degree of dementia who is just about coping in his home environment and who then needs hospitalisation for investigation or treatment. The consequent change of environment, new medication and new routine tips the balance and precipitates an acute confusional state. In this case features of both types of confusion will be present.

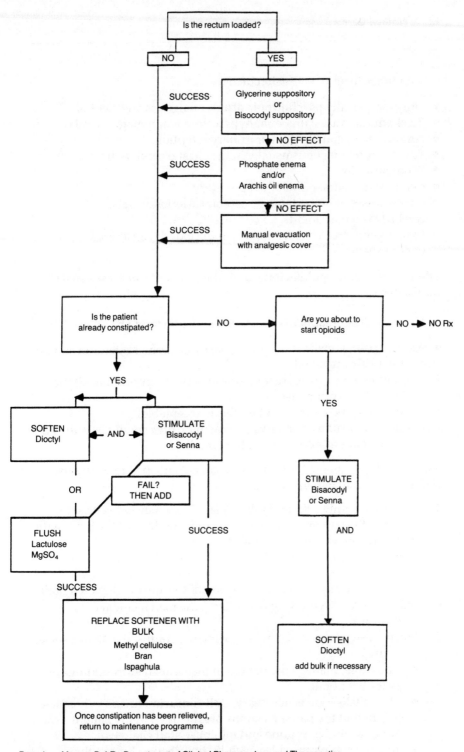

Based on: Morgan D.J.R., Department of Clinical Pharmacology and Therapeutics, Charing Cross and Westminster Medical School, University of London. (Unpublished)

Figure 3.5: Treatment of constipation

Common causes of confusion include:

- Drugs: especially psychotropic drugs, analgesics and alcohol.
- Biochemical causes: uraemia, hypercalcaemia, hypoglycaemia.
- Anoxia, pain, constipation or urinary retention.
- Toxins: from infections usually in the chest or urinary tract.
- Following a fit.
- Cerebral tumours: primary or secondary.
- Other causes of brain damage: cerebral arteriosclerosis, cerebrovasular accidents.
- Psychogenic: from depression or, in the elderly, an altered environment.

Often confusion is multifactorial and more than one of these causes is implicated.

Treatment: The treatment of reversible causes should be attempted:

- Anoxia, pain, constipation and urinary infection or retention should be effectively managed.
- Chest infections can be treated, this may not be appropriate if the quality of life is otherwise poor.
- Sedation may be reduced, when this is acceptable.
- The dose of insulin or oral hypoglycaemic drugs should be reduced to match the patient's diminished food intake.

The overall management of confusion is then aimed at reducing the distress caused to patient and family.

1   **Drugs** have only a limited role to play. They may help either by sedating the patient or, by reducing the 'flooding' of the brain with normally unconscious material, allow the patient to feel less completely out of control. But many confused patients require no medication, indeed sedative drugs can actually worsen the confusion by depressing the function of the already depleted brain cells. (*See* Box 3.8 for drugs of value in the management of confusion.)

2   **Practical steps** are aimed at increasing the confused patient's sense of security.
    - If possible, manage the patient in the familiar surroundings of their own home.
    - If hospitalisation is necessary, or if confusion occurs in hospital, ensure that the patient's family are included in the patient's care. Adopt a familiar routine and minimise staff changes.
    - In either setting provide a well-lit, quiet room. Ensure that hearing aids, glasses, clocks and calendars are working and correct.

3 **Communication**
- Attempt to increase the patient's contact with reality by explaining who you are, where they are, what day it is.
- Avoid confrontation or collusion, but meet the patient at an appropriate emotional level. For example:

  'The hospital is on fire – I must get out of here.'
  'That sounds very frightening, as though you are trapped.'
  'That's just how I feel'.

  This kind of response helps to break the vicious circle of confusion and isolation causing fear and agitation, increasing confusion and isolation.
- Confusion is contagious. Family and staff need a clear explanation of the cause(s) of the patient's confusion and need to be involved, both separately and together, in discussions on management. This is another occasion when the multidisciplinary approach is needed.

By understanding something of the factors and background that may lead to patients becoming confused, pharmacists can help families to cope with a sad and most disturbing situation. Also, by reinforcing the idea that the patient has not gone mad, but that this is another result of the disease process, some of the anguish in the situation can be removed.

If a patient becomes confused his medication should always be reviewed (*see* Box 3.9). Pharmacists could usefully inform the doctor if the patient is on any drug known to cause confusion.

Insomnia

The amount of time that people sleep varies. It is important to check previous sleep patterns and to discover if the main difficulty is getting to sleep, waking during the night or waking too early in the morning. Someone used to working an early shift for years may continue to be wide awake by 4.00 a.m. even though they are now retired or ill.

Patients with a far advanced illness may suffer from insomnia due to physical problems such as cough, itch, pain or nocturnal frequency. Anxiety or depression frequently disturb sleep. Night sweats sometimes respond to an indomethacin suppository or Indocid R, 75 mg given at night. Insomnia improves as these symptoms are relieved.

Although hypnotics should be prescribed for the shortest possible period and should probably be used intermittently, tolerance and dependency are often irrelevant in treating those with a very short life expectancy. However, the continued prescription of hypnotic drugs

Box 3.8: Drugs of value in the management of confusion

Indications	Individual drugs	Dose	Special features
Agitated confusion	Chlorpromazine (IM) Methotrimeprazine (SC)	Initial: 25–100 mg Maintenance: 25–50 mg tds	Methotrimeprazine more sedating
	Haloperidol	Initial: 10–20 mg IM(SC) Maintenance: 5–20 mg p.o.	High incidence extra-pyramidal side effects
	Diazepam	Initial: 5–10 mg PR Maintenance: 5–15 mg nocte	Risk of dependency with continuing use
	Chlormethiazole	Initial: 2–3 caps p.o. Maintenance: 1–2 caps 4 hourly	Where confusion due to alcohol withdrawal
Paranoid confusion	Trifluoperazine	2–4 mg tds	Where agitation not a feature
	Chlorpromazine	25 mg tds	Where agitation a feature
Nocturnal restlessness/ confusion	Thioridazine	25 mg 5 p.m. 50 mg 9 p.m. (1 a.m. dose pm)	Minimal extra-pyramidal side effects
	Chlormethiazole	1 cap 5 p.m. 2 caps 9 p.m. (1 a.m. dose pm)	Short acting – no 'hangover' effect

---

Box 3.9: Drugs that can cause confusion include:

Psychotropic drugs
Pentazocine
Indomethacin
Digoxin
Beta-blockers
Diuretics

Atropine, hyoscine
Anti-Parkinson drugs
Sulphonamides
Phenytoin
Cimetidine

---

should be reviewed just as carefully and regularly as any other medication. Hypnotics should only be prescribed after careful assessment and the failure of other approaches to the problem. But if they are required, the following can be used:

1   Temazepam (Normison, Euhypnos) 10 to 30 mg at night. This is a short-acting benzodiazepine with little risk of cumulative sedation. However, benzodiazepines should be used with caution in agitated patients, and their use could result in a disinhibitory effect which could be equally distressing to the patient. Nitrazepam can result in a hangover effect in patients with renal insufficiency.
2   Chlormethiazole (Heminevrin) is said to be a good hypnotic for the elderly as it is unlikely to precipitate or increase confusion. The usual dose is two capsules (or 10 ml), at night, but a further capsule can be given with benefit earlier in the evening or, if the patient is restless, in the night.

Alcohol remains a good hypnotic, especially for the elderly. Antidepressant drugs given at night to depressed patients will improve their sleep pattern. The person who has taken barbiturates for years should be allowed to continue.

Night sedatives are often given too late. In some patients who get distressed a small dose (of alcohol or chlormethiazole) given at 6.00 p.m. can act as a 'sundowner'. Then after a peaceful but not a drugged evening, a further dose can be given at 9.00 or 10.00 p.m. as a 'nightcap'. This prevents the patient becoming increasingly agitated through the evening as he looks forward with dread to another disturbed night.

Sometimes just a sense of security, following admission to a hospice for example, allows a patient to sleep well for the first time for weeks. It may be kind to point out to families, guilty at having been unable to cope at home, that this is partly because the patient is no longer having to worry about being a burden to them.

Other symptoms

Pharmacists may be asked for advice on conditions such as sore mouth and urinary incontinence. Information on the likely causes and possible treatments are presented in tabular form in *Appendix D*.
Pharmacists are often involved in the supply of medicated dressings for terminal patients. A useful reference is:

Thomas, S. 1990. *Wound Management and Dressings*. Pharmaceutical
    Press, London
1991. The Antimicrobial Properties of Two Metromidazole Medicated Dressings
    Used to Treat Malodorous Wounds. *Pharm J* **246**: 264–6

Crisis points

The course of a terminal illness from the first sign of the fatal disease and ending with death is often marked by crisis points.
    Continuous support throughout the course of a long drawn-out disease is usually not practical, but if there is an awareness of possible times of crisis, and these times are *anticipated*, then the patient and his family have a better chance of completing their hard journey with some dignity and success.
    Pharmacists are in a good position to follow the stages of a family's progress, to look out for times of particular stress and, where appropriate, to suggest that help is needed and from where it should be sought. A suggested list of potential crisis points in a (cancer) patient's illness, together with possible reactions to each particular situation is given in Box 3.10.

Conclusion

By understanding the disease processes and possible lines of treatment for patients with advanced disease, pharmacists can take their place as full members of the multidisciplinary team caring for terminal patients in the community.
    In addition, pharmacists should make themselves aware of the strengths and weaknesses of medical and social services in their area. Familiarity with admission criteria and procedures for the local hospice or palliative care unit will provide a comprehensive understanding of local terminal care facilities.

Box 3.10: Potential crisis points for (cancer) patients

First symptom	'Should I worry my husband?'	PANIC
Medical appointment	'I don't think the doctor knows either.'	UNCERTAINTY
Hospital investigations	'No one looked at me.'	LONELINESS
Diagnosis	'Don't tell him doctor, he'd give up if he knew.'	ISOLATION
Treatment	'I can't face another course.'	DREAD
Side effects	'Why should this happen to me?'	ANGER
Remission	'They *say* everything's all right.'	ANXIETY/ DEPRESSION
Appearance of secondary	'Who has failed: treatment, doctor or me?'	FAILURE
Loss of function	'I can't even wash myself'	DEPENDENCY
Stopping treatment	'The doctors said nothing more could be done.'	ABANDONMENT
Hospice	'Dead End or Place of Hope?'	FEAR

Further reading

Drug and Therapeutics Bulletin, 1990. **28**: (5) 97

Geriatric Medicine, 1987. **17**: (4) 35–9

Geriatric Medicine, 1987. **17**: (5) 63–6

Palliative Medicine, Edward Arnold; *Journal of Pain and Symptom Management*, Elsevier. Both these journals contain valuable articles reviewing various methods of symptom control and other topics in terminal care.

Baines M. 1990. *Drug Control of Common Symptoms*. St Christopher's Hospice (Booklet)

Cody, M. 1990. Depression and the Use of Antidepressants in Patients with Cancer. *Palliative Medicine* **4**: (4) 271–8

Regnard, C.F.G. & Davies, A. 1986. *A Guide to Symptom Relief in Advanced Cancer*. Haigh and Hochland, Manchester

Saunders, C. & Baines, M. 1989. *Living with Dying*. 2nd Edition. Oxford University Press, Oxford

Saunders, C. (Ed) 1984. *The Management of Terminal Malignant Disease*. Edward Arnold, London

Sykes, N. 1990. *The Management of Nausea and Vomiting*. The Practitioner **234**: 286–90

Twycross, R.G. & Lack, S. 1986. *Therapeutics in Terminal Cancer*. Churchill Livingstone, Edinburgh

4 Pharmaceutical Aspects of Pain Control

Graham Sewell

Pharmacists working with clinicians in the control of cancer pain must be aware of the range of analgesic preparations and drug delivery options available to them. Pharmacists should also have a clear grasp of formulation issues associated with various dosage forms to ensure the safe and effective use of analgesic medicines, particularly in the case of strong opioid analgesics.

The analgesic ladder

The range of analgesic preparations required in the relief of cancer-associated pain is defined by the World Health Organisation (WHO) three-step analgesic ladder (*see* Fig. 4.1).

Treatment of pain usually begins with a non-opioid analgesic (or sometimes a NSAID such as naproxen). If this becomes ineffective, a weak opioid such as codeine or dextropropoxyphene (Co-proxamol) is prescribed. If weak opioids fail to control the pain or if adverse effects appear, a further step up the ladder to a strong opioid is required.

The non-opioid analgesic preparations on the lower rung of the three-step analgesic ladder are familiar to most hospital and community pharmacists. A wide range of commercially manufactured solid-dose formulations (including generic preparations) is available for oral administration. Dispersible tablet and oral liquid formulations are available for patients with swallowing difficulties. Some NSAIDs are available as suppository formulations, for example naproxen suppositories, 500 mg. Examples of non-opioid analgesics for oral use include aspirin, paracetamol and naproxen.

Similarly, a wide range of weak opioid preparations is available to meet the requirements of the second rung of the analgesic ladder for the treatment of persistent mild to moderate pain. Codeine is formulated as the phosphate salt in tablets of 15, 30 and 60 mg strengths and as a syrup at a concentration of 5 mg/ml. A codeine phosphate injection is also

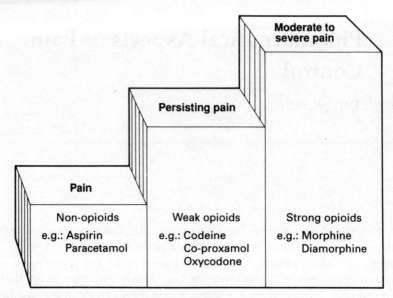

Source: Marie Curie Cancer Care Research Book

Figure 4.1   The WHO three-step analgesic ladder

available but this preparation is unlikely to be used in the relief of cancer-related pain. Co-proxamol tablets contain 32.5 mg of dextropropoxyphene hydrochloride (a weak opioid) and 325 mg of paracetamol.

The range of doses of non-opioid and weak opioid analgesics used in clinical practice is shown in Box. 4.1.

The final step on the analgesic ladder refers to the so-called 'strong' opioids group of which morphine and diamorphine are used to treat more severe forms of cancer pain. In this context it is recognised that the aetiology of the pain is more important than the severity per se. Commercially manufactured and hospital 'special' preparations of morphine and diamorphine are used as both oral and parenteral formulations. Examples of commercial preparations are shown in Box 4.2. It is sometimes necessary to combine parenteral doses of diamorphine with other drugs, for example antiemetic agents. The formulation, drug stability and compatibility issues associated with the strong opioids tend therefore, to be more complex than is the case with analgesics on the lower two rungs of the WHO ladder.

Morphine and diamorphine

The stability of the two drugs in aqueous solution differs markedly.

In aqueous solution, diamorphine degrades rapidly by sequential

Box 4.1: Range of doses used in clinical practice

Non-opioid analgesics

Drug	Strength	Dose	Comment
Aspirin dispersible BP	300 mg	300–600 mg 4–6 hourly	Useful adjunct in bone pain. Gastric irritant
Paracetamol tablets BP	500 mg	0.5–1 g 4–6 hourly	Lack of gastrointestinal effects

Weak opioids

Drug	Strength	Dose	Comment
Codeine Phosphate tablets BP syrup BP	15/30/60 mg 25 mg/5 ml	15–60 mg 4 hourly	Approximately 1/12th as potent as morphine
Dihydrocodeine tablets BP elixir	30 mg 10 mg/5 ml	30–60 mg 4 hourly	Approximately 1/10th as potent as morphine
Dextropropoxyphene capsules BP	equivalent of 65 mg HCI salt	one capsule 4–8 hourly	Accumulation occurs, especially with poor renal function.
Dextropropoxyphene and paracetamol (co-proxamol)	32.5 mg each 325 mg tablet	2 tablets 4–8 hourly	Dose intervals may have to be increased in the elderly

hydrolysis of the 3 and 6 acetyl esters to give 6-acetyl morphine and eventually morphine[1]. Diamorphine is most stable in the pH range 4–5, but because the rate of hydrolysis is dependent upon ionic strength it is not possible to include buffer salts in oral liquid formulations[2].

**Box 4.2: Examples of strong opioid analgesics for oral and
parenteral use**

Oramorph concentrated oral solution (20 mg/ml) + calibrated dropper

Oramorph oral solution (10 mg/5 ml)

MST tablets (controlled-release morphine sulphate) available as
10 mg, 30 mg, 60 mg, 100 mg and 200 mg tablets

SRM – Rhotard tablets (controlled-release morphine sulphate)
available as 10 mg, 30 mg, 60 mg and 100 mg tablets

Sevredol tablets (instant release morphine sulphate) available as
10 mg and 20 mg tablets

Diamorphine hydrochloride for injection, available as 5 mg, 10 mg,
30 mg, 100 mg and 500 mg strengths (freeze-dried powder in vials)

Morphine on the other hand degrades slowly by oxidation in aqueous
solution to give morphine N-oxide and pseudomorphine[3].
Consequently, morphine is the analgesic of choice for oral liquid
formulations, where either the hydrochloride or sulphate salt is used.

Morphine preparations

A commercially available oral liquid formulation of morphine sulphate is
manufactured in strengths of 10 mg in 5 ml and 20 mg in 1 ml. A
calibrated dropper is supplied for the administration of the concentrated
solution. Both solutions are pleasantly flavoured and have a shelf life of
up to two years at an ambient temperature. Hospital-prepared oral
liquid formulations of diamorphine are occasionally used to control
cancer pain. These are usually simple formulations of diamorphine
hydrochloride in chloroform water but the shelf life is limited to one
month by the poor stability of diamorphine in aqueous solution[1].
However, in clinical terms, because of the analgesic potency
of the degradation product, no diminution in efficacy of analgesia is
likely to be encountered.
    A potential disadvantage of the oral morphine solution is that a
4-hourly dose frequency is often required to prevent pain breakthrough.
Conversely, a potential advantage is the possibility of four hourly

assessment to allow adjustment and stabilization of dose.

Controlled-release tablets of morphine sulphate are a more convenient alternative to oral solutions since the dose frequency is 12-hourly. The MST 'Continus' tablet comprises a matrix of morphine sulphate with hydroxyalkyl cellulose and a higher aliphatic alcohol. The higher aliphatic alcohol slowly dissolves in gastric juices to expose hydroxyalkyl cellulose granules onto which the morphine sulphate is adsorbed. On contact with gastrointestinal juices the hydroxyalkyl cellulose hydrates and the morphine sulphate diffuses from the matrix[4].

MST tablets containing, 10, 30, 60, 100 and 200 mg morphine sulphate are available. The bioequivalence of MST tablets with oral morphine solutions has been established and doses are equivalent. A patient may be transferred from oral liquid morphine to controlled-release morphine sulphate tablets by giving the same 24-hour dose of morphine but divided into two 12-hourly doses[5]. For example, a 20 mg dose of oral morphine solution every 4 hours would equate to one 60 mg MST tablet every 12 hours.

Instant release morphine sulphate tablets, Sevredol, are available in 10 mg and 20 mg strengths.

Strong opioid treatment normally commences with oral morphine solution, which is later replaced by controlled-release morphine sulphate tablets when the dose required to relieve pain has been established. Traditional complex oral formulations such as 'Brompton Cocktail' which contain cocaine and alcohol have no place in modern pain control. The use of a multiplicity of ingredients in the 'cocktail' meant that the need to increase one ingredient resulted in unnecessary increases in others, including cocaine. Oral analgesia is the preferred option for most cancer patients although parenteral analgesic administration is required for patients with dysphagia, intractable vomiting or profound weakness.

Parenteral formulation of diamorphine

Despite its poor stability in aqueous solution when compared with morphine, diamorphine is the strong opioid of choice for parenteral formulation. The greater solubility of diamorphine salts when compared with morphine salts facilitates a smaller injection volume and allow higher analgesic doses to be given without practical difficulties. The relative aqueous solubilities of diamorphine and morphine salts are as follows:

- Diamorphine hydrochloride: 1.0 g dissolves in 1.6 ml of water
- Morphine sulphate: 1.0 g dissolves in 21 ml of water
- Morphine hydrochloride: 1.0 g dissolves in 24 ml of water

In view of the poor stability of diamorphine hydrochloride in aqueous
solution, the injection is commercially available in vials containing
sterile, freeze-dried powder. These are reconstituted under aseptic
conditions with either 0.9% sodium chloride injection or water for
injection BP. High strength diamorphine injections tend to be
hypertonic and cause pain at the site of injection. For this reason
diamorphine injections of strengths greater than 500 mg should be
reconstituted with water for injection[1].

Ambulatory infusion devices

An alternative to intermittent subcutaneous injection of diamorphine is
the use of miniaturised ambulatory pumps to give a continuous infusion
of the drug normally via the subcutaneous route. Several ambulatory
devices are now available, all with different attributes and running
costs. The Baxter Multiday Infuser (see Fig. 4.2a) is a disposable device
which is used for up to five days and then discarded. The drug infusion
is driven out of the elasticated infusion reservoir through a flow
restrictor and because it has no batteries it is very light and comfortable
for the patient to wear.

The Graseby MS26 Syringe Driver (Fig. 4.2b) is probably the most
common device in current clinical use for pain control. The medication
reservoir is a pre-filled disposable plastic syringe, which is normally
changed on a daily basis. The pump has a low battery alarm and is worn
in a holster on the patient's abdomen. For ambulatory patients the
holster can fit snugly on the shoulder.

The Parker Micropump (Fig. 4.2c) is one of the most advanced devices
available. It is very small and light, largely by virtue of an external
programming module. It is worn under the clothing in a belt holster and
has a pen-type bolus inject button which enables the patient to self inject
a pre-programmed 'top-up' dose.

The Pharmacia Deltec CADD PCA device (Fig. 4.2d) is another
computerized ambulatory infusion pump. The pump has a dedicated 50
or 100 ml cassette and is driven by a 9 volt battery. A 50 ml cassette can
provide a patient with diamorphine for up to two weeks.

In addition to the purchase cost of each device, the running costs
including consumables such as medication reservoirs, batteries, but
excluding drugs, are also given in Box 4.3. A 5-year 'write-off' time
would be realistic for the non-disposable Graseby, and Parker and
Pharmacia devices.

Although the disposable Baxter Multiday Infuser is the most costly
device over each month in use, there is no capital cost associated with its
purchase. It is essential that subcutaneous catheters and not butterfly

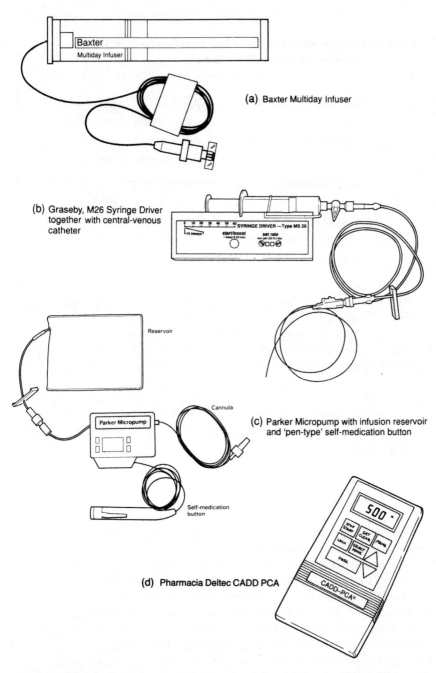

(a) Baxter Multiday Infuser

(b) Graseby, M26 Syringe Driver together with central-venous catheter

(c) Parker Micropump with infusion reservoir and 'pen-type' self-medication button

(d) Pharmacia Deltec CADD PCA

Source: (b), (c) Allwood, M and Wright P. 1991. *The Cytotoxics Handbook*. Radcliffe Medical Press, Oxford

Figure 4.2   (a) Baxter Multiday Infuser; (b) Graseby MS26 Syringe Driver; (c) Parker Micropump; (d) Pharmacia Deltec CADD PCA

**Box 4.3: Comparative purchase and running costs of four
            ambulatory infusion devices**

(a)	Baxter Multiday Infuser	Purchase price: approx. £25
		Cost/month: approx. £150
(b)	Graseby MS26 Syringe Driver	Purchase price: approx. £450
		Cost/month: approx. £8
(c)	Parker Micropump	Purchase price: approx. £2000
		Cost/month: approx. £60
(d)	Pharmacia Deltec CADD PCA	Purchase price: approx. £2500
	(patient controlled analgesia)	Cost/month: approx. £65

needles are used with ambulatory pumps for continuous subcutaneous
infusion as they are more comfortable for the patient.

When using ambulatory infusion pumps it is necessary to ensure that
the diamorphine infusion is stable, not only under refrigerated storage
conditions prior to use but also under 'in-use' conditions when the
temperature of an infusion in a pump worn under the patient's clothing
may reach 37°C. Recent stability studies[6] have shown that diamorphine
infusions in water for injection may be stored at 4° C for up to 14 days
and are stable over 7 days under in-use conditions at 37° C with less than
5% degradation of the drug.

Admixtures

In some cases it is clinically desirable to infuse diamorphine with an
antiemetic drug and it has become common practice to include the
antiemetic with diamorphine in the same syringe. Extreme caution is
necessary to avoid physical incompatibilities, which result in drug
precipitation and chemical incompatibilities which result in the
degradation of one or both drugs in the admixture. Stability studies on
admixtures of diamorphine with haloperidol and cyclizine, commonly
used antiemetics, have shown that the major factor leading to
incompatibility is the relative concentration of each drug. Cyclizine
100 mg/15 ml is compatible with up to diamorphine HCl 1.5 g/15 ml;
cycline 150 mg/15 ml is compatible with up to diamorphine HCl 150 mg/
15 ml, at room temperature for 7 days. Haloperidol 10 mg/15 ml is
compatible with diamorphine HCl up to 1.5 g/15 ml at room
temperature for 7 days.[7] The presence of cyclizine reduces the stability

of diamorphine by 40% at ambient temperatures. Refrigeration has been found to improve the stability of diamorphine in prefilled syringes. Great care needs to be taken when considering combinations of diamorphine and cyclizine. The compatibility of diamorphine with cyclizine and metoclopramide and methotrimeprazine is summarised in Box 4.4 (based on a range of concentrations of diamorphine/antiemetic mixtures[8]).

Box 4.4: Compatibility of diamorphine/antiemetic admixtures over 24 hours at ambient temperature[8]

Admixture	Chemical stability	Physical stability
Diamorphine HCl + metoclopramide	+	+
Diamorphine HCL + methotrimeprazine	+	+
Diamorphine HCL + cyclizine lactate (< 10 mg/ml)	+	+
Diamorphine HCl + cyclizine lactate (> 10 mg/ml)	+	−

Conclusion

The use of syringe pumps to administer opioids by continuous subcutaneous injection can be performed most efficiently if the syringe contains quantities of the drug to provide sufficient for 24-hour administration in a single syringe. The inclusion of an anti-emetic drug in the syringe provides further convenience for staff and patient. If pre-filled syringes can be provided which have an extended shelf-life, the opportunity for treatment of patients at home is enhanced.

It is likely that future developments in pain control, including circadian drug-delivery to exploit the patient's biorhythms and the infusion of more active opioid metabolites such as morphine-6-glucuronide, will depend on the use of ambulatory pumps. Pharmacists should maintain a current awareness of literature reports concerning drug stability and compatibility issues associated with the use of these devices.

Boxes 4.5 to 4.7 provide summarised information on common questions regarding pain control; rational treatment of pain; and co-analgesics and cancer pain. Fig. 4.3 contains a compilation of reasons why drugs, including analgesics, may not have their anticipated effect; these issues should be of particular interest to pharmacists.

Box 4.5: Summary of questions which may arise regarding control of pain

Problem	Pharmacological principles	Practice
1 Which drug for very severe pain?	Efficacy, not potency, matters	Use pure agonists (morphine, diamorphine)
2 Will individuals need different doses?	Individual variation in responses to be expected	Start with small doses, work up quickly until pain is controlled
3 How should doses be spaced?	1 Range of effective plasma concentrations; 2 shape plasma time-concentration curve; 3 cumulation; 4 physiology of pain	Either give four–five times daily or use a sustained release formulation; 2 No 'as required' scripts
4 Route of administration?	1 Shape of plasma time–concentration curve; 2 respiratory depression	Remember toxicity at plasma peak
5 Is methadone an alternative?	Cumulation	Avoid methadone
6 Can opioid drugs be mixed?	1 Single receptor mechanism; 2 partial agonism and antagonism	No gains expected from opioid combinations, and possible loss of analgesia
7 Will the dose have to be increased progressively? Will this cause respiratory depression?	1 Fact of tolerance; 2 nature of tolerance	Be prepared to increase dose to control pain
8 Will dependence occur? Will there be withdrawal reactions?	Nature of dependence in those who suffer pain	Forget it, except when withdrawing drug and then taper dose gently
9 Will there be unwanted drug effects?	1 Spectrum of opioid effects; 2 physiological antagonism; 3 potentiation	1 Use mixtures with antiemetics; 2 Combat constipation with anticipation
10 Are there not ethical problems?		Treat for what remains of life, not for death, but let death be a normal part of life
11 Will the solutions keep on the shelf?	Facts about solubility and stability of drugs	1 Shelf-life of each solution or combination of solutions to be considered individually; 2 storage conditions

Adapted from: Vere, D.W. Ed 1978. In: *Topics in Therapeutics 4*. The Pharmacology of Morphine Drugs used in Terminal Care, Edinburgh, Churchill Livingstone

Box 4.6: The rational treatment of pain

Cause of pain	Primary treatment	Secondary treatment	Further treatment
Visceral from involvement of abdominal pelvic organs	Analgesics may help	Low-dose steroids	Coeliac axis block for abdominal pain. Intrathecal block for pelvic pain
Bone pain	1 Palliative radiotherapy; 2 Non-steroidal anti-inflammatory drugs; 3 Immobilisation e.g. Cervical collar or pinning	Analgesics	Nerve block. Low-dose steroid may help
Soft-tissue infiltration	Analgesics	Low-dose steroids and NSAIDs may help	Nerve block
Nerve compression	Analgesics	High-dose steroids	Nerve block
Secondary infection • Deep	Systemic antibiotics including metronidazole if possibility of anaerobes. Local surgery	Analgesics	Nerve block
• Superficial	Systemic antibiotics. Local applications e.g. povidone iodine		
Pleural pain	Antibiotics if appropriate	Analgesics	Intercostal block
Colic due to bowel obstruction	Faecal softeners. Antispasmodics, e.g. loperamide (Imodium)	Analgesics	
Lymphoedema	Analgesics. Intermittent positive pressure machine	High-dose steroids may help	Diuretics rarely of use
Headaches from raised intra-cranial pressure	High-dose steroids. Raise head of bed	Avoid opioid analgesics if possible	Diuretics may help
Pain in paralysed limb(s)	Physiotherapy and regular movement of limb(s) by nurses	Non-steroidal anti-inflammatory drugs	Muscle relaxants

Reproduced from: Saunders, C. and Baines, M. 1983. *Living with Dying*. Oxford University Press

Box 4.7: Co-analgesics and cancer pain

Type of pain	Co–analgesic
Bone pain	aspirin 600 mg 4-hourly or flurbiprofen 50–100 mg b.i.d. or naproxen 500 mg b.i.d.
Raised intracranial pressure	dexamethasone 2–4 mg t.i.d.–q.i.d.
Nerve pressure pain	dexamethasone 2–4 mg daily–b.i.d. prednisolone 5–10 mg t.i.d.
Superficial dysaesthetic pain	amitriptyline 25–100 mg nocte
Intermittent stabbing pain	valproate 200 mg b.i.d.–t.i.d. or carbamazepine 200 mg t.i.d.–q.i.d.
Gastric distension pain	Asilone, Maalox Plus 10 ml p.c. and nocte, metoclopramide 10 mg 4-hourly
Rectal tenesmoid pain	chlorpromazine 10–25 mg 8 to 4-hourly
Muscle spasm pain	diazepam 10 mg nocte, or baclofen 10 mg t.i.d.
Lymphoedema	diuretic–not usually effective
Infected malignant ulcer	metronidazole 400 mg t.i.d. or clindamycin 300 mg q.i.d.

Reproduced from: Twycross, R.G. and Lack, S.A. 1983. *Therapeutics in Terminal Cancer*, Edinburgh, Churchill Livingstone

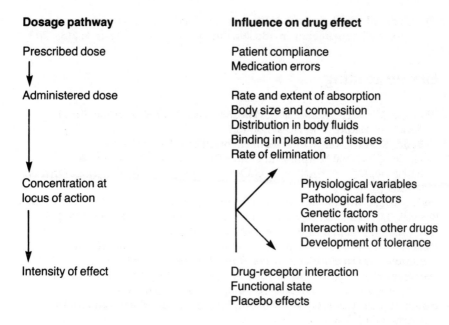

Dosage pathway	Influence on drug effect
Prescribed dose	Patient compliance
	Medication errors
Administered dose	Rate and extent of absorption
	Body size and composition
	Distribution in body fluids
	Binding in plasma and tissues
	Rate of elimination
Concentration at locus of action	Physiological variables
	Pathological factors
	Genetic factors
	Interaction with other drugs
	Development of tolerance
Intensity of effect	Drug-receptor interaction
	Functional state
	Placebo effects

Reproduced from: Koch-Wesser, J. Serum Drug Concentrations as Therapeutic Guides. *New England Journal of Medicine* 287, 227–31, 1972.

Figure 4.3 Reasons why drugs may not have their anticipated effect

References

(1) Bruce Scott, D. (Ed) 1988. *Diamorphine, its Chemistry, Pharmacology and Clinical Use.* Woodhead-Faulkner, London

(2) Beaumont, I.M. 1982. Stability Study of Aqueous Solutions of Diamorphine and Morphine using HPLC. *Pharm J* **229**: 39–41

(3) Connors, K.A., Amidon, G.L. & Stella, V.J. 1984. *Morphine* (Monograph). In: Chemical Stability of Pharmaceuticals, 2nd edition. John Wiley & Sons, Chichester

(4) 1984. *The Continus System.* Information booklet. Napp Laboratories, Cambridge

(5) 1991. Prescribing in Terminal Care: Guidance on prescribing section. *British National Formulary* **Number 22**. British Medical Association/Royal Pharmaceutical Society of Great Britain, London

(6) Northcott, M., Allsopp, M.A., Powell, H. & Sewell, G.J. 1991. The Stability of Carboplatin, Diamorphine, 5-fluorouracil and Mitozantrone Infusions in an Ambulatory Pump Under Storage and Prolonged 'In-use' Conditions. *J. Clin. Pharm. Ther.* **16**: 123–129

(7) Allwood, M.C. 1991. The Stability of Diamorphine Alone and in Combination with Anti-emetics in Plastic Syringes. *Palliative Medicine* **5**: 330–333

(8)   Regnard, C., Pashley, S. & Westrope, F. 1986. Anti-emetic/Diamorphine
       Mixture Compatability in Infusion Pumps. *Br. J. Pharm. Pract.* **8**: 218–220

Further reading

1989. *The Edinburgh Symposium on Pain Control and Medical Education*. Royal
    Society of Medicine Services, London
    Budd, K. Advances in the Treatment of Chronic Pain 111–118
    Hanks, R.G. Oral Morphine in Cancer Pain: Fact and Fiction 39–46
    Radstone, D.J. & Crowther, A.G.O. The Appropriate Use of Syringe Drivers
    99–107
1991. Syringe Drivers Still Causing Problems, Pharmacists Told. *Pharm J* **247**: 210
Beswick, D.T. 1987. Use of Syringe Driver in Terminal Care. *Pharm J* **239**: 656–8
Doyle, D. 1990. Pain Control. *The Practitioner* **234**: 283–5
Hanna, M.H. *et al*. 1991. Disposition of Morphine – 6-Glucuronide and
    Morphine in Healthy Volunteers. *British J of Anaesthesia* **66**: 103–7
Hassenbusch, S.J. *et al*. 1990. Constant Infusion of Morphine for Intractable
    Cancer Pain Using an Implanted Pump. *J Neurosurgery* **73**: 405–9
Hoskin, P.J. & Hanks, G.W. 1990. Morphine: pharmacokinetics and clinical
    practice. *Br J Cancer* **62**: 705–7
Lipman, A.G. 1990. Drug Therapy in the Management of Pain. *Br J Pharm Pract*
    40: 22–9
Oliver, D. 1991. Syringe Drivers in the Community. *The Practitioner* **235**: 18–80
Ventafridda, V. & Conno, de F. 1990. NSAIDs as the First Step in Cancer Pain
    Therapy: Double-blind Within-patient Study Comparing Nine Drugs. *J of
    International Medical Research* **18**: 21–29
Currently out of print: Tempest, S.M. 1989. The Control of Pain in Terminal
    Malignant Disease. Napp Laboratories, Cambridge

5   Community Pharmacists and Terminal Care

Barbara J. Stewart

A specialised form of the 'extended role'

Community pharmacists are in an ideal position to contribute positively to the care of terminally ill patients in the community. Preceding chapters have described how the hospice philosophy of care can be applied in the home setting. Effective palliative care requires the most appropriate use of medicines coupled with an understanding of the total needs of dying patients and their families. Pharmacists should be concerned with all aspects of the drug-use process and provide comprehensive pharmaceutical care, not just the supply of medicinal products. Key activities include:

- maintaining appropriate stock levels of opioid analgesics;
- responding to requests for unusual drugs and obtaining stocks within an appropriate timescale;
- dispensing prescriptions for terminal patients promptly;
- delivering dispensed medicines and appliances to patients' homes, when requested (domiciliary contact);
- advising patients, families and carers; patient counselling to help compliance;
- liaising with members of the home care team;
- communicating with GPs (alerting GPs when symptom control appears inadequate or when problems arise with usage of certain dosage forms).

Pharmacists' involvement in palliative care of terminally ill patients in the community can be seen as a very specialised form of the community pharmacist's 'extended role'. It need not be linked to providing pharmaceutical services to a hospice, although for a number of community pharmacists this will have provided a route into active involvement in terminal care in the community. The following pages describe the variety of ways in which community practice provides opportunities for involvement with terminal patients.

Identifying terminal patients in the community

The fact that a patient is in the terminal stages of an illness can be brought to the attention of the community pharmacist in a number of ways. The patient's GP may contact the pharmacy to enquire about the availability of a prescription item, probably an opioid analgesic, often explaining the urgency of the situation. Similarly, contacts may be made by other health care professionals, for example members of the home care team.

It is worth noting at this point the importance for carers of the terminally ill to be able to obtain supplies of medicines used in terminal care. If a pharmacist believes he or she is dispensing for someone who may be terminally ill, communication with the GP can reveal the likely drug treatment and allow stocks to be ordered in advance. In some areas pharmacists who are prepared to keep stocks of drugs used in

Box 5.1: Examples of prescription items for terminal patients	
Drug category	**Drug product**
1 Anti-cancer drug	Tamoxifen (Nolvadex) Aminoglutethimide (Orimeten) Megestrol acetate (Megace)
2 Opioid analgesic	MST Continus tablets Diamorphine injection Morphine elixir
3 Laxative	in high doses (softeners–often laxative of choice)
4 Anti-nauseant anti-emetics	Prochlorperazine (Stemetil) Metoclopramide (Maxolon) Domperidone (Motilium)
5 Unusual products rarely used except in hospice context:	Diazepam suppositories Midazolam injection Methotrimeprazine (Nozinan, tablets formerly named Veractil) Ondansetron (Zofran) Dexamethasone tablets – in high doses

terminal care have made this known to local Macmillan nurses. thus saving carers and nurses inconvenience.

Opportunistic identification of terminal patients is possible in the pharmacy, for example, through the types of prescriptions being presented (*see* Box 5.1), the purchase of special feed items (Ensure and Fortisip); or by apparently innocuous questions from family members or carers 'Will he kill himself taking morphine?', 'He is on a high dose of morphine. Will he become an addict?'

Helping to achieve compliance

Palliative care relies strongly on the most effective use of a range of medicines and flexible dosage regimes. Patient counselling can help achieve optimum compliance. Explaining why and how preparations should be taken or used when treatment is started will help the terminal patient and family or carers. Reinforcing the dosage regime for pain control is especially important. Analgesics should not be given on a PRN basis, that is, only after the pain has returned. This is undesirable in the case of chronic pain of cancer. The patient's and family's understanding of this principle will greatly assist one major aspect of palliative care. Pain breakthrough indicates the need for a medication review.

Pharmacists are involved with patients and their families and also liaise with the 'home care team'. Sometimes the pharmacist may be required to give reassurance to families or patients themselves – this may take place in the pharmacy or sometimes in the patient's own home. Medication, bulky feeds or oxygen may need to be delivered to the home. The family may need assistance in organising supplies so that essential equipment and medication do not run out. It can be reassuring for patients and families to know that a pharmacist can be contacted by telephone to give advice in times of emergency.

Using traditional pharmaceutical expertise

Knowledge of different dosage forms is important, especially when patients have difficulty in swallowing. In these circumstances liquid preparations or dosage forms for rectal administration are often required.

Many of the drugs in terminal care are used rarely and may be available only as unlicensed 'specials'. Pharmacists may not be required to compound extemporaneous preparations themselves, but can call on supply sources, for example pharmaceutical manufacturing specialists or local hospital pharmacy departments. Using these expert facilities for special formulations can ensure that products are prepared to high standards and are promptly obtained. Time can be an important factor when patients are in the final stages of their terminal illness.

Others involved in the drug supply chain are pharmaceutical wholesalers and manufacturers. Pharmacists involved in terminal care will develop a special rapport with these suppliers, who will appreciate their special needs, perhaps for unusual products, often required at very short notice.

Of fundamental importance is the pharmacist's understanding of pain relief and his or her knowledge of analgesic products. This can include non-opioid analgesics presented in a variety of dosage forms, and the use of opioids in syringe drivers.

Being aware of new products and advising prescribers of their potential in terminal care can be a useful contribution by the pharmacist. A recent example is the introduction of metronidazole gel, a product used in the treatment of malodorous wounds. The drug information bulletin *Care of the Dying*, distributed by MEREC is an excellent source of advice and information on commonly occurring problems in palliative medicine, where drug therapy has a role.

Case studies

The following case studies illustrate the contribution of community pharmacists towards the home care of several terminal patients.

Case one

Mr P was a man in his late fifties whose wife had presented a prescription for dispensing at her local community pharmacy. The pharmacist noticed that an unusually high dose of dexamethasone tablets 2 mg had been ordered – six tablets a day (dexamethasone tablets can be dissolved in warm water if required. This could be helpful for patients like Mr P). When explaining to Mrs P the need for Mr P to take the dose once a day, it was obvious that Mrs P was in a highly agitated state. The pharmacist was immediately alerted to Mrs P's heightened emotional state and gave her the opportunity to talk about the situation, if she wished, by asking if the prescription for her husband attracted a charge and if so, whether a prepayment certificate had been considered. Further explanation was given as to how a prepayment certificate would help if a variety of drugs were to be required in the forthcoming months.

Mrs P's attitude indicated she was angry and upset but responded to the pharmacist's active listening by confiding that her husband's illness had just been diagnosed as carcinoma and that he was terminally ill. The pharmacist was naturally sympathetic although Mrs P continued to express anger about the situation.

The following day, Mrs P returned to the pharmacy, sought out the pharmacist and apologised for her outburst the previous day. The understanding and sympathetic approach shown by the pharmacist resulted in Mrs P visiting the pharmacy regularly during the following months for her husband's prescriptions. Sometimes the pharmacist's personal advice was sought, sometimes not. The pharmacist had made sure that Mrs P was aware of her availability for advice and guidance whenever it was required. More specifically, medication for Mr P was provided with detailed instructions so that the maximum benefit relevant to her husband's terminal condition was achieved.

Case two

Miss B was an elderly, frail woman who was a regular customer at her local pharmacy. One day she appeared at the counter somewhat confused, enquiring about the possibility of purchasing food supplements for her sister who was known to live with her. On gently questioning Miss B, the pharmacist was able to find out that Miss B's sister had been discharged from hospital recently and was seriously ill at home.

The pharmacist advised Miss B that it was possible for her GP to order these special foods, Ensure or Fortisip, on a prescription under certain circumstances, and that this would be financially beneficial to her. Miss B was encouraged to discuss the matter with the GP or the visiting nurse as soon as possible. The pharmacy would obtain the foods promptly and ensure future supplies, should they be required.

Through this simple enquiry the pharmacist was alerted to the possibility of Miss B's sister being in the terminal stages of her illness.

Case three

Mr R was a 79-year-old patient known to be in the last few weeks of his terminal illness, carcinoma of the lung. The local pharmacy had supplied oxygen to his home throughout his illness (oxygen cylinder, cylinder head and mask).

Nebulisation therapy was prescribed in the form of Ventolin nebules, after it had been established by the prescriber that the nebulisation therapy would produce at least a 20% difference in expiry rate flow from the lungs. The pharmacist visited the home of Mr R, demonstrated how the contents of the Ventolin nebule should be used in the end well of the mask and ensured that the rate of oxygen flow was 4 litres per minute (*see* note below). Mr R and a family member confirmed their understanding of how to continue the nebulisation therapy using the Ventolin nebules and were given further reassurance by being told to contact the pharmacist by telephone should any problems arise.

Note: the pharmacist was aware that the rate of flow of oxygen from a conventional oxygen cylinder – 4 litres per minute as above – was not ideal but that the particular circumstances of Mr R did not lend themselves to the purchase of an electric nebuliser (retail price approximately £140; not included in Drug Tariff, therefore not available on NHS prescription). A bobbin flow gauge used in conjunction with a cylinder, often used in a hospital or hospice setting would be another alternative for securing a more effective flow rate of oxygen. However, availability of bobbins in community practice is limited.

Case four

Mr J, a widower in his late sixties had been receiving palliative care for approximately two years since being diagnosed as suffering from cancer of the colon/rectum. He lived alone in sheltered accommodation, was independent and self-sufficient and managed with occasional admissions to the local hospice.

His medication was provided routinely by his local pharmacist, who made occasional deliveries to his home. But frequently Mr J gave the pharmacist advance notice of his requirements and visited the pharmacy when the items were ready for collection.

The range of medication prescribed for Mr J (in a one month period) was as follows:

Aldactone tablets 50 mg	ї mane
Betnovate RD ointment	use 2–3 daily
chlorpromazine tablets 25 mg	її tds
Coloplast bags	
Comfeel Protective Film Sachets	
Hirudoid gel	Use tds
Hygroton tablets 50 mg	її mane
lactulose solution BP	10 ml bd
Limone ostomy deodrant spray	
morphine mixture 40 mg/5 ml	10 ml qqh, 20 ml nocte
Ranitidine tablets 150 mg	ї bd
sodium picosulphate elixir 5 mg/ 5 ml	15 ml nocte
Stemetil tablets 5 mg	ї tds
temazepam capsules 20 mg	ї nocte
Tubigrip bandage	
Ventolin inhaler	її puffs qds prn
Voltarol retard tablets 100 mg	ї12 hourly

Pain control was achieved with oral morphine solution, which started, 2 years earlier, as morphine sulphate 10 mg/5 ml, dose 5–10 ml qds and had been gradually increased to morphine sulphate 40 mg/5 ml dose 10 ml qqh, 20 ml nocte. An excellent relationship developed between Mr J and the pharmacist. The pharmacist was able to advise on many aspects of the multifarious drug regime and encourage compliance. For his part, Mr J commented as follows:

'Some pharmacists are very helpful, including Mr W (community pharmacist) and it is shown in their attitude. It can be a problem finding pharmacists who keep stocks of morphine. Having to wait or return for the preparation can be difficult to cope with, especially when you are living on your own. Some pharmacists don't understand at all and are not helpful. Mr W is not like that'.

Clearly there is room for community pharmacists to increase their understanding of the needs and difficulties of terminal patients particularly regarding supplies of opioid analgesics.

Professional interaction

The involvement of pharmacists with terminal patients can and should result in interaction with members of the primary care team and the specialist home care team.

An initial contact may often be with a GP, who is not necessarily known to the pharmacist personally and who is not familiar with the legal requirements for prescribing a controlled drug. More frequent contact is likely to take place with home care nurses. The district nurse is often involved at the outset and community pharmacists could be involved with the ongoing supply of dressings. Specialist nurses such as Macmillan nurses are likely to be part of the home care team and play an active role in maintaining pain relief.

Pharmacists involved in terminal care will be aware of the potential role of social workers but perhaps will not have had direct contact with this group of professionals. Occasionally, relatives are referred to the pharmacy by the hospice social worker.

Because of the emotional and spiritual dimensions in terminal care, pharmacists may occasionally find themselves in situations where it is appropriate to refer patients or relatives to a priest, chaplain, rabbi, or other spiritual adviser.

Coping with emotional aspects

It is well-recognised that professionals involved in terminal care have to cope with their own emotions related to death and dying. Community pharmacists and their staff sometimes have to cope with the emotional aspects of communicating with terminal patients and their families.

Staff should be trained to recognise distressed patients or relatives, to treat them sympathetically and always to call the pharmacist. Staff should listen and be sympathetic but would not be encouraged to give advice.

Staff members can feel emotional but it is possible to develop mechanisms for coping with distressed or tense people. Listening, being sympathetic and offering practical advice where appropriate can be helpful under such circumstances.

Communication

The following section applies generally to issues associated with communication in the health care setting and has relevance to aspects of community practice.

Difficulties in communication in terminal situations are a great cause of emotional distress. They occur because people are uncertain about how to talk to dying patients, and so withdraw from them, leaving them feeling isolated.

Psychological defence mechanisms

People facing adversity may use various defence mechanisms to ward off distressing thoughts and feelings. These mechanisms are unconscious and are almost universal in dying patients. Denial is probably the most common mechanism used by the dying patient, and can sometimes operate in stages (*see* reference to the work of Kubler-Ross, Chapter 2). For the dying patient, a degree of dependency on other people is inevitable and appropriate. Some people show exaggerated dependency while others stubbornly resist help. Sometimes, dying patients deal with powerful emotions by displacing them onto other people, for example unreasonable anger may be directed against professional staff, causing distress in the recipient. Pharmacists need to be aware of this possibility.

The value of listening and giving information

Anxious or depressed patients need an opportunity to express their worries and ask questions about their illness and its likely effect on their lives. Patients may well want more information about the purpose of medication. Pharmacists should not underestimate a patient's capacity for understanding medical matters but care should be taken to avoid giving explanations in unnecessarily technical language.

Referral to patient medication records held in the pharmacy can be invaluable in assembling information for terminal patients.

Before giving information, it is important to find out what patients know already and what aspect of their treatment is causing them the most worry. Patients should feel that they have undivided attention and that their concerns are taken seriously. There is often a gulf between what has actually been said and what the patient hears. Because of their anxiety, some of what they are told will not be remembered and important points should be repeated or written down. When speaking in the pharmacy, an attempt should be made to avoid distractions and being overheard by moving to a quiet spot – something which is also practised for other forms of patient counselling on sensitive issues.

All these actions should help to put patients at their ease. Time spent in finding out what the patient knows and believes is also likely to improve his or her cooperation with treatment.

Reassurance is important and can help to dispel unnecessary fears both in patients and their families. But care should be taken not to give false reassurance by making light of real problems. The pharmacist's approach should be sympathetic and concerned – a professional approach – but should avoid creating an over-intense relationship with the patient, which could breed dependency.

The following interpersonal skills have direct relevance to communicating with terminally ill patients or their family members:

- developing a relationship that inspires confidence in patients and conveys a feeling of interest and concern;
- interacting in a non-judgmental manner;
- recognising and being attentive to the patient's emotional needs;
- being alert to and interpreting non-verbal cues from patients.

Non-verbal communication

Non-verbal communication provides messages and expresses feelings that are not subject to direct conscious analysis by the people involved in the communication. A number of factors combine to make it likely that most patients will be sensitive to the non-verbal communication of health practitioners. First, illness generally provokes fear, anxiety and emotional uncertainty. Under these circumstances, many patients will have a strong need for others to help them define their situation and understand their feelings. Secondly, most patients are likely to be searching for factual information about the nature of their disease even if some information has been provided already such as at the time of diagnosis, by medical staff.

Patients are likely to express emotions in non-verbal ways, especially through facial expressions. A patient may be experiencing severe pain, fear or depression for the first time and thus be unable to describe these emotions in words. It is probable, therefore, that patients will communicate a significant amount of important information through their own non-verbal cues. This valuable information can be lost if the pharmacist is insensitive by not being open to non-verbal communication. People vary in how well they understand such things as facial expression, voice tone and body movements. In particularly embarrassing situations, patients may be able to control their facial expressions but may 'leak' their true feelings through body movements.

Communication between members of the primary health care team is important; if positive expectations can be transmitted to the patient, real benefits may follow. In areas such as pain management, which have relatively strong psychological components, expectations can significantly influence outcomes. Patients are most likely to obtain the information on which these expectations are based, through non-verbal cues. It is now recognised that practitioners' interpersonal effectiveness is related to their non-verbal expressive skills.

One of the most influential non-verbal cues is *gaze*. People generally know and respond when they are being looked at and know when somebody is avoiding eye contact. Also the gaze of a person may indicate something about the patient's mood. *Voice tone* can clearly express emotion and is relatively easy for patients to detect. Feelings like fear, anger, sadness, joy and pain are readily transmitted through vocal cues.

A major category of non-verbal communication involves *body positions and gestures*, for example posture, hand movements, gait, lean, foot tapping etc. Although not much is known about the meaning of such individual actions in isolation, they have important effects on the 'immediacy' of an interaction. Direct orientation and forward lean help to convey a feeling of concern.

One of the most critical aspects of communication is the degree of consistency between verbal and non-verbal cues. The slightest inconsistency is likely to be noticed in seriously ill patients. The degree and type of inconsistency between verbal and non-verbal cues create 'innuendo' which can be either comforting or unhelpful to an ill person depending upon the situation.

Bereavement

Pharmacists are likely to come into contact with family members and carers not only during the terminal stages of a patient's illness but in the bereavement period following the death. The difficulties in communication outlined above apply equally to communication during bereavement. A resumé of aspects of bereavement is provided in Appendix E.

Future developments

Recent developments in patient care in the community have included the use of modern technology in the form of ambulatory infusion pumps. This has led to improvements in pain control and in some cases in effective home-based cytotoxic chemotherapy.

A working party of the Royal Pharmaceutical Society (January 1990) has considered the role of the community pharmacist in cytotoxic cancer chemotherapy; terminal care; enteral nutrition; and diabetic therapy. The summary of recommendations to the report is provided in Appendix F. Referring to terminal care, the Society advocates community pharmacists becoming more involved in the treatment of cancer patients, particularly those being treated by continuous infusion; and in playing a greater part in the supply of medicines for the treatment of the terminally ill. Greater liaison is called for between hospitals and community pharmacies and it is suggested that community pharmacists should provide pre-filled syringes and supply equipment such as syringe drivers for domiciliary use (analogies are made to the existing arrangement for supplies of oxygen equipment). The working party report does not elaborate on the mechanism for such supplies.

Clearly, these activities would be dependent upon the inclusion of syringe drivers in the Drug Tariff; on pharmacists' willingness to undertake the activity, including domiciliary visits; on pharmacists acquiring appropriate knowledge and skills; and by provision of remuneration for the service provided. At present, syringe drivers in domiciliary use are on loan from local hospitals or the Macmillan service or they belong to local GP surgeries.

This special extension to the existing pharmaceutical service provided by community pharmacists could become a reality in the foreseeable future. The service may well be provided by some, but not all, community pharmacists who have an interest in terminal care and who have undertaken education and training activities in the subject area.

Ambulatory infusion devices, especially syringe drivers, are likely to play an important part in the development of home-based symptom control. Details of practical applications and the use of the Graseby syringe driver are provided in Appendix G.

The working party report has advocated greater communication between hospitals and community pharmacies, so that pharmacists can be informed when a patient is discharged into the community. Health authorities, for their part, have been considering the whole question of terminal care. Health authorities through the National Association of

Health Authorities and Trusts (NAHAT) have published revised guidelines in the report of a joint advisory group *The Care of People with Terminal Illness* (December 1991). The report details principles of good terminal care and components of a comprehensive service for the dying. Health authorities will need to make informed policy decisions to ensure that the best use is made of available resources and that effective coordination takes place between the National Health Service and the voluntary and charitable bodies which principally fund the hospice services. Health Authorities have a key role in taking account of the quantity and quality of the services provided in their districts, and the needs and opinions of both the users and providers of terminal care. Regional Health Authorities need to keep in touch with developments at district level, while the Department of Health has a role in ensuring the provision of clear national policies and central initiatives as required.

With greater recognition being given to the important challenge of terminal illness and the current reorganisation of health services, the opportunity exists to ensure that the dying are always treated with dignity and respect. Pharmacists can make their contribution towards this aim through better understanding of the concepts involved in palliative care of the terminally ill; increased knowledge of symptoms and their management; application of appropriate knowledge and skills; and insight into communication with patients and their families.

Appendix H contains information on existing courses, video tapes and journals on many aspects of terminal care.

Further reading

Working Party Report, 1990. Home Chemotherapy. *Pharm J* **244**: 93, 108–9
1990. Most Patients with Cancer Pain can be Treated at Home. *Pharm J* **244**: 195
Me.Rec. 1991. *Care of the Dying*. Drug Information Letter No. 82. The Medicines Resource Centre, Liverpool
Calnan J. 1984. *Talking with Patients*. William Heinemann, London
Hanks, G. & Kandela, P. *The Management of Cancer Pain*. Clinical Dialogue Series. Pacemaker Medical Publishing, England
Hargie, O. 1986. *A Handbook of Communication Skills*. Croom Helm, London
Lugton, J. 1987. *Communicating with Dying People and their Relatives*. Austen Cornish Publishers, London
Twycross, R.G. & Lack, S. 1988. Oral morphine. *Information for Patients, Families and Friends*. Beaconsfield Publishers, Beaconsfield

6 Legal Aspects of Controlled Drugs in Terminal Care

Alan Stears

This chapter deals with the impact of the Misuse of Drugs legislation on community pharmacists who are involved in the treatment of terminally ill patients.

Misuse of Drugs Act

Although the Misuse of Drugs Act is a rather draconian piece of legislation, banning the production, supply and possession of around 200 substances, several of which are widely used in medicine, specific provision is made in Section 7 of the Act for subsidiary legislation (currently the Misuse of Drugs Regulations 1985). The regulations minimise interference in the provision of bona fide pharmaceutical services. Consequently, apart from a limited number of drugs which have no recognised place in the treatment of disease or injury (the present list consists of 21 drugs such as cannabis and LSD), pharmacists need no special permits or authority to handle any of the drugs controlled under the Act.

Levels of control

Different levels of control are imposed under the legislation, depending on the perceived level of danger from the drug concerned. The specially-designated drugs have the strictest controls imposed on them under Schedule 1 of the Misuse of Drugs Regulations, but this is not likely to be relevant for the treatment of terminal illness. Schedule 2 drugs include the principal opioids and cocaine, while buprenorphine (Temgesic) and most barbiturates fall into Schedule 3. Schedule 4 drugs consist mainly of the benzodiazepines. The lowest level of control, Schedule 5, covers the low dose and dilute preparations of some of the Schedule 2 drugs (e.g. codeine, dextropropoxyphene).

An alphabetical list of the status of the drugs and preparations most likely to be encountered is given in Box 6.1. The status of other compounds should be checked in the current edition of the *Medicines, Ethics and Practice Guide* from the Royal Pharmaceutical Society.

Box 6.1			
Controlled drug	**Schedule category**		
	2	**3**	**5**
buprenorphine		★	
codeine oral preparations			★
Cyclimorph	★		
dextromoramide	★		
DHC Continus			★
diamorphine	★		
Diconal	★		
dipipanone	★		
Fortral		★	
methadone	★		
morphine	★		
MST Continus	★		
Narphen	★		
Oramorph concentrated solution	★		
Oramorph oral solution			★
oxycodone	★		
pentazocine		★	
pethidine	★		
phenozocine	★		
Sevredol	★		
SRM-Rhotard	★		
Temgesic		★	

Prescriptions

Regulation 15 of the Misuse of Drugs Regulations 1985 requires that prescriptions for Schedule 2 or Schedule 3 drugs must be completed in the following manner:

1   written in ink in the prescriber's own handwriting, and signed and dated by him;
2   state the name and address of the person for whose treatment it is issued;

3   specify the preparation and *its form* in every case, and the strength
    where appropriate;
4   specify the dose to be taken;
5   specify the total number of dosage units or the total quantity of
    preparation *in words and figures.*
    Private prescriptions *must* include the issuing doctor's address.
Examples of prescriptions are illustrated in Figure 6.1.

The restrictions on the authority of medical practitioners to prescribe
cocaine, diamorphine and dipipanone under the Misuse of Drugs
(Notification of and Supply to Addicts) Regulations 1973, does not apply
in cases of terminal care, even if the patient has been an addict. The
Home Office has indicated that action under Section 13 of the Misuse of
Drugs Act (relating to irresponsible prescribing) would only be
considered in a case of bona fide prescribing for terminal care, where the
drugs were being diverted for illicit use.

Dispensing

Regulation 16 of the Misuse of Drugs Regulations 1985 governs the
dispensing of prescriptions issued for Schedule 2 or 3 controlled drugs.

1   Such prescriptions must comply with Regulation 15 of the
    Regulations (*see* page 76).
2   They must be issued in the United Kingdom (not in the Channel
    Islands, Eire or Isle of Man) by a doctor on the UK Medical Register.
3   The pharmacist must *either* recognise the doctor's signature *and* have
    no reason to doubt that it is genuine, *or* satisfy himself that it is
    genuine.
4   The prescription must not be dispensed *before* the specified date, or
    later than 13 weeks after the specified date.
5   At the time of supply the pharmacist must mark the prescription
    with the date of supply and retain the prescription at the pharmacy
    until it is dispatched to the Pricing Bureau (NHS prescriptions) or for
    two years (Private Prescriptions).
6   When presented with an incomplete prescription pharmacists have
    to make a professional decision. There is no statutory provision for
    the dispensing of an invalid prescription, but pharmacists would
    want to avoid causing unnecessary distress or discomfort to a
    terminal care patient. Providing the pharmacist took all appropriate
    steps to have the deficiencies in the relevant prescriptions rectified
    as soon as practicable, it seems most unlikely that any action would
    be taken against him or her for dispensing a genuine, unambiguous
    but incomplete prescription, where a delay would have caused
    distress or discomfort to the patient.

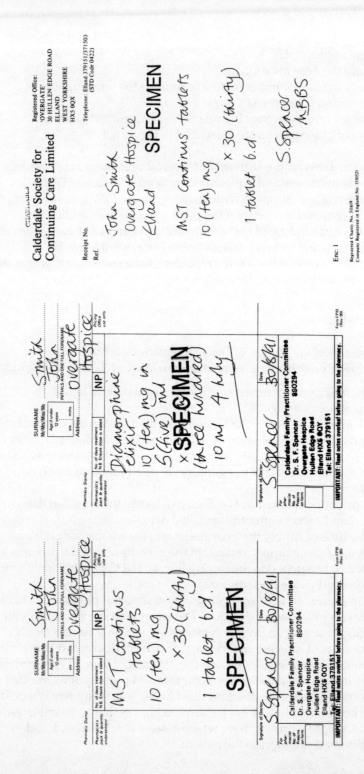

Figure 6.1   Prescriptions for controlled drugs

Delivery by third parties

Dispensed items

Terminal patients being cared for in their homes will have their
medication prescribed on FP10 forms by their GPs. Few terminal care
patients will be in a position to regularly visit the pharmacy to collect
their medication, but the Misuse of Drugs Regulations authorise anyone
'engaged in conveying the drugs' to deliver prescribed drugs to patients.
The pharmacist should ensure that the person claiming to be collecting
the drug on behalf of the patient is bona fide, and the reverse of the
prescription form should be appropriately endorsed. Similarly, if the
pharmacist arranges for someone (e.g. a member of his staff) to deliver
the drug to the patient, it would be prudent to obtain a record of receipt
from the patient's attendant.

Supplies on signed orders

Where third parties are used to deliver requisitioned controlled drugs,
specific requirements in the Misuse of Drugs Regulations must be
complied with. The pharmacist must not pass the drug over to a
messenger unless an authority signed by the recipient is produced for
the pharmacist and retained by him or her and the pharmacist is
reasonably satisfied that it is genuine.

Security

All Schedule 2 controlled drugs (except quinalbarbitone) and two
Schedule 3 drugs (buprenorphine/Temgesic and diethylpropion/
Apisate, Tenuate Dospan) must be kept in the standard safe custody
cabinet unless the police approve alternative arrangements.

  Although there is no evidence to suggest that thieves target
pharmacies likely to be holding large stocks of controlled drugs, such as
those supplying hospices, it would be prudent to obtain advice from the
local Police Crime Prevention Officer. They will often advise the
installation of a safe or a more robust security cabinet than the standard
models.

Returned prescriptions

Regulation 6(2) of the Misuse of Drugs Regulations allows a patient or
his or her representative to return a dispensed controlled drug to *any*
pharmacist for the purposes of destruction. The normal requirement for
destructions to be witnessed by a police officer, Royal Pharmaceutical

Society Inspector etc, does not apply in these cases, but a sensible precaution against possible unsubstantiated allegations of diversion would be to record the destruction and have it witnessed, perhaps by another staff member.

Recycling

There is no *requirement* under the Misuse of Drugs Regulations for drugs returned by patients or their representatives to be destroyed. In the unlikely event of returned drugs being taken into stock, they must be recorded as a receipt in the controlled drug register.

Regarding 'recycling' or 're-use of medicines', the Code of Ethics of the Royal Pharmaceutical Society contains specific guidance on the subject as follows:

'A pharmacist should not dispense for any patient a medicine previously dispensed for another patient and subsequently returned to a pharmacy from a patient's home.'

This guidance applies to all dispensed medicines, including controlled drugs.

Supplies to hospices

Since April 1991 the supply of drugs to hospices has been changed. The new scheme is designed to avoid the difficulties of prescribing where a Hospice Medical Director has no FP10 prescribing rights, and to minimise the costs to hospices of purchasing supplies of drugs.

Hospices will now be able to make arrangements for the provision of full pharmaceutical services, including the supply of drugs, with the local Health Authority. It is envisaged that supplies would be made from a convenient hospital or community pharmacy to the hospice at Health Authority expense, subject to agreement on the range of drugs and services to be supplied and the appropriate cost and quality controls.

Once the arrangements are in place, it should only be necessary for a general medical practitioner to prescribe drugs on form FP10 where the drug required was not in stock and could not be otherwise supplied without unacceptable delay.

Further advice

More detailed information and further interpretation of the Misuse of Drugs legislation can be obtained from the Regional Offices of Home Office Drugs Branch as follows: for enquiries from East Anglia, London and Southern England contact 50 Queen Anne's Gate, London SW1H 9AT (telephone 071-273-3530); for enquiries from South West England, the Midlands and Wales contact P.O. Box 26, Bristol BS99 7HQ (telephone 0272-276736); for enquiries from Northern England and Scotland contact Dudley House, 133 Albion Street, Leeds LS2 8PN (telephone 0532-429941)

References

Medicines, Ethics and Practice: A guide for pharmacists. Current edition. Royal Pharmaceutical Society of Great Britain

April 1991. *The supply of Drugs to Hospices.* Letter EL(91)60. NHS Management Executive

1991. Return of Controlled Drugs to Pharmacies. Council Guidance *Pharm J* **247**: 223

The Misuse of Drugs Act 1971

The Misuse of Drugs Regulations 1985

1991. Pharmaceutical Services to Hospices. *The NPA Supplement* **744**: 1, 3

British National Formulary: Guidance on prescribing – controlled drugs and drug dependence (current edition)

7 Cancer Pain Relief and Palliative Care: An International Perspective

Barbara J. Stewart

Discussion in the preceding chapters has focused on the provision of palliative care in the UK and on pharmacists' involvement with patients at a local level. However the subject has consequences worldwide as each year 4.3 million people die of cancer. This amounts to 10% of all deaths. In countries such as Japan and the United Kingdom, the proportion caused by cancer is as high as 25%. Pain is a common problem. Data from 32 published reviews suggest that 70% of patients with advanced cancer have pain as a major symptom. Of those still undergoing anticancer therapy, some 30% have pain. Reports from developed countries indicate that from 50 to 80% of patients do not receive adequate relief. These figures form the basis of the estimate by the World Health Organisation (WHO) that every day at least 3.5 million people are suffering from cancer pain.

This is a tragedy because reports from several centres indicate that, in 80 to 90% of patients, cancer pain can be controlled completely and that, in most of the remainder 'acceptable relief' is possible. The reasons for this divergence between demonstrated possibility and actual performance are many. The most important ones include:

- A lack of recognition that established methods already exist for cancer pain management.
- A lack of systematic teaching of medical students, doctors, nurses and other health care workers about cancer pain management.
- Fears concerning 'addiction' in both cancer patients and the wider public if strong opioids are more readily available for medicinal purposes.
- Non-availability of necessary pain relief drugs in many parts of the world.
- A lack of concern by most national governments.

WHO programme

Pain and symptom control is one of the priorities of the cancer control programme of WHO; others include prevention of cancer, early diagnosis and curative treatment, and the implementation of national cancer control programmes.

For many years to come, in the absence of totally effective measures for prevention, early diagnosis and curative treatment of cancer, and sufficient health facilities and trained health care workers, active supportive care will be the only realistic, humane approach for many patients. Nothing would have a greater impact on the quality of life of these patients, than the dissemination and implementation of knowledge already available in relation to pain and symptom management.

The WHO Expert Committee on Cancer Pain Relief and Active Supportive Care met in Geneva in July 1989 and has since published a technical report – 804 Cancer Pain Relief and Palliative Care (WHO, Geneva, 1990). The purpose of the Expert Committee was to review the current status of cancer care and pain relief and to produce recommendations and guidelines for improving the quality of life of cancer patients. Recommendations contained in the Report, to Member States, are reproduced in Appendix I.

Earlier draft guidelines of the WHO on the relief of cancer pain expressed the view that, through the use of a limited number of drugs, pain relief was a realistic target for the majority of cancer patients. It was recognised that cancer pain had been commonly undertreated and frequently neglected as a public health problem. Freedom from pain should be seen as the right of every cancer patient and access to pain therapy should be regarded as a measure of respect for this right. A goal of the WHO is freedom from cancer pain as soon as possible. There is also a need for greater understanding of 'palliative care' and within this the use of analgesic drugs.

If current trends continue, cancer mortality is expected to rise in nearly all regions of the world. The ageing factor makes a positive contribution to figures for expected changes in deaths from cancer.

In most parts of the world, the majority of cancer patients present themselves with far-advanced disease. For these, the only realistic option is palliative care, including pain relief. Palliative care, therefore, must be a high priority.

Opioid availability

The importance of orally administered opioids cannot be overestimated and there must be sufficient quantities available. Greater availability of strong opioids has allowed more cancer patients to be cared for at home, with no associated increase in illicit drug use.

In many countries, morphine and codeine are not available for treatment of cancer pain, or are available but underused. As a result, many cancer patients suffer pain needlessly. The WHO is attempting to address these problems by promoting a wider knowledge among health care workers of the importance of orally administered opioids in the management of cancer pain and by encouraging drug regulatory authorities to make sufficient quantities of these substances available to treat patients in their own countries.

The Single Convention on Narcotic Drugs, 1961, is the international treaty that regulates the production, manufacture, import, export and distribution of narcotic drugs for medical use, including the opioids. It also sets the framework for concerted international action against illicit manufacture and production, and against the diversion of narcotic drugs from licit to illicit markets. Countries party to the Single Convention are required to control all aspects of the use of opioids within their territories and all international movement of opioids.

An International Narcotics Control Board (INCB) is established in Vienna, Austria, and together with the WHO has developed a joint working document focused on a series of issues related to the supply and demand for opioids for medical purposes and related practical problems.

Guidelines for cancer pain management have been prepared and are now widely disseminated. These emphasise that a small number of relatively inexpensive drugs are the mainstay of pain management. Field testing has demonstrated the efficacy of the guidelines in the vast majority of cancer patients. At present the guidelines are available in 15 languages and further translations are being prepared.

Risk of diversion

Many years and much effort have gone into developing an international system to prevent diversion, with the emphasis on combating illicit traffic. Even so, the international treaty does not aim to reduce the use of opioids that are needed for medical care. However the Convention specifically recognises 'the medical use of narcotic drugs continues to be indispensible . . . and that adequate provision must be made to ensure their availability'.

Fear of diversion of opioids into illicit channels is often ill-founded, since only a very small percentage of illicit drugs come from the health care system. In particular, orally administered morphine is not a drug of choice for opioid-dependent persons. Nevertheless, concern about illicit drug use and its social consequences has curtailed the availability of opioid drugs to patients with cancer pain.

Sweden is a good example of a country where the greater availability of strong opioids, especially preparations for oral administration, has allowed more cancer patients to be cared for at home. Equally important is the fact that there has been no associated increase in illicit drug use or diversion of drugs to established addicts.

Risk of psychological dependence from medically prescribed opioids

There is very little published information assessing drug abuse and the risk of psychological dependence (addiction) for patients who receive opioid analgesics for any type of painful chronic illness. Data suggests that the medical use of opioids is rarely associated with the development of psychological dependence.

A series of studies reporting the abuse of analgesics in patients with chronic illness found that abuse of non-opioid analgesics or combinations of weak opioids and non-opioids was more common than abuse of more potent opioids. Drug use alone is not the major factor in the development of psychological dependence, as other medical, social, psychological and economic factors play an important role.

Tolerance to opioids

There is evidence to suggest that patients receiving opioids on a continuing basis develop some degree of tolerance to the analgesic effect of these drugs. Physical dependence also occurs, as demonstrated by the appearance of withdrawal symptoms following the administration of an antagonist such as naloxone, and by reports of acute withdrawal symptoms in patients who stop drug therapy abruptly after pain-relieving neurolytic or neurosurgical procedures. Considering patterns of drug use in cancer patients, progression of metastatic disease causing increasingly severe pain is the major factor determining the need to increase analgesic dosage. Tolerance to the different opioid effects develops at different rates.

When orally administered, strong opioids are used in the manner described by the WHO, tolerance is only rarely a practical problem. Similarly, physical dependence does not represent a clinical problem. Opioid drugs should not be stopped abruptly but withdrawn slowly to prevent the onset of the signs and symptoms of withdrawal. In short, tolerance and physical dependence are pharmacological effects that occur with repeated drug administration. They are to be distinguished from psychological dependence which is a behavioural pattern characterised by compulsive drug-seeking behaviour leading to an overwhelming involvement with the use and procurement of the drug.

Availability of other drugs for the relief of cancer pain

Problems may also arise in the cases of diazepam, and buprenorphine, which is on the list of basic drugs for cancer pain relief but which is controlled under the Convention of Psychotropic Substances, 1971. When implemented as intended, the Convention should not restrict the availability of therapeutically useful substances. In practice, however, impediments and disincentives to the prescription and supply of such medicines can occur if legal controls are unduly onerous and bureaucratic.

'The Convention gives high priority to the continuing availability of the therapeutically useful substances it covers, but where legal controls are unduly onerous and bureaucratic, impediments and disincentives to their prescription and supply do occur in some countries.'

Many countries have additional problems of drug supply and distribution, which affect the availability of medicines in all therapeutic categories but which are not related to the international control of drugs. Non-availability of medicines in these countries is often due to a combination of factors such as inadequate funding of government health services, lack of health care infrastructure, and inadequate facilities for storage and distribution of medicines. These problems are being addressed by the WHO, through its Action Programme on Essential Drugs. This programme recommends, among other measures, the establishment of national drug policies and the adoption of national costs of essential drugs, based on the WHO Model List of Essential Drugs. When such policies are formulated, it is important that they take into account the needs of cancer pain relief programmes. National and local formularies should include sufficient appropriate drugs to allow the guidelines on cancer pain relief to be implemented.

The WHO Expert Committee has concluded that the following steps are necessary on an international scale, to ensure adequate drug availability:

- review of legislation;
- review of administrative practices;
- determination of the probable needs of the country;
- review of legislation and practices that may affect the availability of other drugs.

Networks

The WHO is active in establishing a network of supporting individuals and organisations. The immediate objective is to provide basic knowledge about the prevalence of cancer pain and what can be done to relieve it. The long-term aim is to change attitudes about cancer pain management, and to dispel false ideas and fears about pain relief drugs, and to ensure their ready availability to the patients in need.

WHO Collaborating Centres have been established in Amsterdam and Winnipeg (quality of life), Madison (symptom evaluation), Milan (cancer pain), New York (cancer pain research) and Oxford (palliative care). Teaching faculties are being developed jointly with the International Association for the Study of Pain (IASP), International Society of Nurses in Cancer Care (ISNCC) and the International School for Cancer Care (ISCC). A survey of impediments to drug availability has been conducted, together with the International Federation of Pharmaceutical Manufacturers Associations (IFPMA).

Governments are being encouraged to set up statutory cancer control programmes, and to give pain relief a high priority. As a result, for example, India has doubled its federal budget for cancer; the state of Wisconsin, USA has established a state-wide initiative for improving cancer pain management; and in Canada, the Ministry of Health and Welfare has distributed cancer pain relief guidelines.

Pharmaceutical profession

Following publication of the WHO report, two pharmaceutical organisations, International Pharmaceutical Federation (FIP) and the Commonwealth Pharmaceutical Association (CPA), identified with the WHO the need for the following:

1 A simple formulary of oral morphine solutions, particularly for use in Third World countries.
2 Training programmes for pharmacists.
3 A pain syllabus for inclusion in undergraduate pharmacy degree courses.

Progress has been made by FIP/CPA on development of the pain syllabus and it is expected that it will be commended internationally to schools of pharmacy in the near future.

Hospice pharmacy in the United States of America

Based on model programmes developed in England in the 1960s, the
first hospice programmes in the USA were designed to provide a
coordinated programme of palliative and supportive services in both
home and inpatient settings. The hospice has greatly expanded the
scope of the care-giving team to include the family, community
members and many health professionals who participate on an equal
basis. Included on the interdisciplinary team are representatives from
medicine, nursing, social work, allied therapy, clergy, volunteers and
pharmacy. The development of clinical pharmacy has identified the
hospice as a natural practice setting. To date over 600 pharmacists have
been identified as practising hospice pharmacy in America. Areas
covered are the monitoring of drug profiles, dosing of opioids, and the
education of both the patient and hospice team.

The American Pharmaceutical Association (APhA) has added a
section group of hospice pharmacists within the Academy of Pharmacy
Practice and Management for the purpose of developing a network of
practitioners. The National Hospice Organisation representing 1,529
programmes, has recently launched a Council of Hospice Professionals,
which includes a section for pharmacists with the same goal as the
APhA, that will reach pharmacists through hospice programmes.

Pain control in America, apart from psychological and spiritual pain,
is primarily managed through several systems delivering opioids,
nonsteroidal anti-inflammatory drugs and antidepressants. Morphine is
the first line drug of choice. It is delivered in oral concentrate (Roxanol),
long acting tablets (M S Contin) and patient controlled analgesia (pca)
pumps. Dermal patches of fentanyl (Duragesic) are used also (*see* Box
7.1).

Box 7.1	
Roxanol	Manufacturer – Roxane Co. Preparation of morphine sulphate as tablets, liquid and suppositories
M S Contin	UK equivalent MST Continus tablets UK manufacturer – Napp Laboratories
Duragesic	Manufacturer – Janssen Dermal patches available in a variety of strengths

Pharmacists dispensing medication to hospice patients are paid a fee for service. According to a recent survey, cognitive or clinical services are paid under contract 50% of the time. One third of pharmacists responding to the survey indicated that they volunteered their time and the remainder reported a combination of the above.

Further reading

WHO Expert Committee, 1990. *Cancer Pain Relief and Palliative Care*, Technical Report 804. WHO, Geneva

Teoh, N. 1990. Curbing Cancer. *International Pharmacy Journal* 4 (2) 77–8, 4 (3) 115–7, 4 (4) 117–80

Cone, M. 1990. Controlled drugs: Does prevention of abuse lead to prevention of use? *International Pharmacy Journal* 4 (1) 2–3

Twycross, R.G. 1989. *Cancer Pain: A global perspective*. The Edinburgh Symposium on Pain Control and Medical Education, Royal Society of Medicine Services Ltd, London

8 AIDS and its Implications for Palliative Care

Robin Hull

The advent of Acquired Immune Deficiency Syndrome (AIDS) has introduced a new type of patient, often relatively young, who requires palliative care. HIV is no respector of persons and it is increasingly manifesting itself among the heterosexual population. In principle, these patients have similar requirements to other terminally ill patients, but there are a number of specific problems which will be addressed in the chapter.

Background to the syndrome

AIDS was first recognised in homosexual men in San Francisco in 1981. It is now clear that isolated cases of the disease were encountered worldwide for more than two decades prior to this. Since 1981, the spread of AIDS in individual regions of the world has followed a geometric progression which starts slowly and with each doubling increases its rate of growth. There has been a gradual slowing down of this 'doubling time' in regions in which large numbers are now infected. Worldwide, this doubling time is currently about one year.

In Africa, where the infection appears to have originated, the situation is appalling, although poorly documented. Estimates put the number of infected individuals as high as 60% of sexually active adults in some areas of Subsaharan Africa. Currently about one million persons in the US are infected with HIV and the rate of new infections has been increasing by 80,000 annually since 1986.

One very worrying feature of the disease is the way in which the number of cases suddenly increases in countries which were virtually free of the disease. This is currently happening in India and Thailand and is predicted to happen in the Phillipines and Indonesia in the present decade. Recent figures for the UK are shown in Box 8.1, but like all AIDS statistics only represent the tip of the iceberg. The real total of HIV infected persons in the UK could be in excess of 50,000. In the year to December 1990 the number of heterosexually acquired cases rose by

115%, more than twice as fast as among homosexuals where the rise was only 46%. In the face of a gradual rate of increase in the United Kingdom it is easy to be lulled into a false sense of security.

Box 8.1: UK AIDS cases up to end of September 1991 How virus probably acquired				
	Male	**Female**	**Total**	**Deaths**
Sexual intercourse				
between men	3925		3925	2475
between men and women				
'high risk partner'	14	29	43	25
other partner abroad	206	101	307	155
other partner UK	22	15	37	19
Intravenous drug abuser	161	62	226	120
Homosex/bisex and iv drug abuser	79		79	52
Haemophiliac	268	4	272	196
Recipient of blood:				
Abroad	14	26	40	28
UK	15	16	31	22
Child of at-risk or infected parent	17	28	45	22
Other/undetermined	56	7	63	42
Totals	4777	288	5065	3156

Source: Communicable Disease Report (1991). **1**, 41

The virus

AIDS is caused by infection with the Human Immunodeficiency Virus (HIV). This virus is highly specialised and depends for its existence and reproduction on inserting itself into human cells, particularly T4 lymphocytes and to a lesser degree cells within the central nervous system. HIV possesses a special enzyme, reverse transcriptase, which enables it to insert its own genetic code into the DNA of the lymphocyte. Once the virus is within the lymphocyte DNA the host cell becomes a factory for the production of more HIV. Because it is so specialised, the virus is extremely fragile and it is simple to destroy outside the body.

How the virus is spread

Although the virus has been found in many body fluids it is only in the presence of lymphocytes that there is real risk of infection. Lymphocytes are found in blood and also in semen. These two body fluids are the principal means of spread of infection. Human milk may also contain lymphocytes but this is a rare vector for transmission of the virus. Other body fluids are safe *unless* contaminated with lymphocytes from blood or semen. Infection depends upon the entry of T4 lymphocytes from infected persons into the blood of uninfected individuals. Formerly this could occur during blood transfusion or treatment with blood products but now blood is screened (at least in the developed world). Infection can only occur where infected cells enter the recipient's blood by injection through the skin e.g. needlestick, penetration through damaged skin, or through damaged genital mucous membrane caused by trauma or sexually transmitted disease (STD). Sexual transmission occurs more frequently during anal sex, since the rectal mucosa is easily torn, allowing direct transfusion of seminal lymphocytes into the host's blood. It may also occur following oral or vaginal penetration where ulcerative genital or mouth disease pre-exists due to trauma or other causes.

Drug abuse

Injecting drug users have in the past readily shared syringes. Considerable efforts now are being made in the United Kingdom to provide clean, sterile equipment – usually on an exchange basis. In the context of HIV transmission, the nature of the drugs being injected is irrelevant. Sharing allows blood from one user to be injected directly into subsequent users. As the situations in Edinburgh and New York have shown, this is a very efficient means of transmission. There is rising concern over syringe sharing by body builders, who are using intra-muscular anabolic steroids.

Many cases of sexual transmission (including heterosexual) have occurred in non-injecting drug users, where the partner was an injector.

Homosexuals

Homosexual communities have responded to the spread of AIDS with wide changes in sexual practice which have resulted in slowing of the epidemic in this sector of the population. However, some reports, particularly from Amsterdam and London, suggest that there may be some return to former practices.

Heterosexuals

In America there has been a dramatic rise in STDs among heterosexuals while the incidence among homosexual males has dropped sharply. The rise of STDs among certain sections of the heterosexual population is at a higher level than seen in almost 40 years. There is a relationship between transmission of HIV and genital ulcers due to STD.

Worldwide, of 500,000 expected cases of AIDS in 91/92, 40% will be women. HIV may be transmitted to the unborn baby if the mother is infected during or prior to pregnancy.

Risk to health professionals

Accidental transmission from patients to health professionals is extremely rare, although a number of cases of infection have occurred worldwide following needlestick injury. In all cases, however, the incident was noticeably serious with definite amounts of blood being injected into the carer. Considerable caution must be exercised where blood samples are collected from an AIDS/HIV patient. The greatest danger is when a needle is resheathed – an operation which should be avoided if at all possible. There is an even smaller risk of transmission when mopping up blood spills or other contaminated body fluids. The main risk here is when the carer has skin lesions, e.g. abrasions, psoriasis, eczema on the hands. Double gloving is recommended. It should be noted that HIV is not transmitted through coughs and sneezes.

Of course, all health care staff can become infected following sexual contact with an infected partner; and a number of physicians, surgeons, dentists, nurses and pharmacists are known to be infected. However, there is only one definite case of patients being infected by a health care worker. This is where a Floridian dentist infected three patients, one of whom has now died.

Clinical aspects

Infection does not always occur following contact with HIV. Where it does, sero-conversion usually follows between six weeks and six months after infection. However, in some cases, sero-conversion may be delayed for two years. Sero-conversion is the phase of the infection at which HIV antibodies are first released into the blood. It may be associated with a mild influenza-like illness which is often unnoticed by the patient. It is only after sero-conversion that the blood will test positive in standard HIV tests. However, it is not clear whether a person

is infectious in the time between the initial infection and sero-
conversion.

The progression to clinical manifestations of HIV infection, leading to
persistent generalised lymphadenopathy, AIDS related complex, and
AIDS, is very varied in both time and pattern.

There may be progression to the AIDS-related complex (ARC) in
which there is chronic fever with night sweats, malaise and weight loss.
At a later stage there may be persistent generalised lymphadenopathy
(PGL). Progression from either of these HIV related states may occur
with the development of the full syndrome. The characteristic feature of
AIDS is impaired immunity which allows opportunistic infections or
unusual forms of malignancy to develop. Opportunistic infections (OI)
include many viral, bacterial, fungal and protozoan diseases which are
normally rare in immunocompetent individuals. HIV also has a direct
effect on certain cells in the brain, giving rise to dementia in some
patients.

Palliative care of AIDS patients

This differs little from the palliative care of cancer: good communication,
skilful symptom control and appropriate support of the family are
essential. Counselling poses additional problems because of the youth
of many people with AIDS. The possibility of dementia (normally so rare
among this age group) and potential cross-infection may give rise to
special problems. Counselling is complicated by the highly critical
attitudes of society towards AIDS. Counselling has two main aims: first
to reduce the spread of HIV and secondly to reduce the psychological
effect of being infected with the virus. Education directed at avoidance
of infection is a vital part of preventive care of all health care workers. It
depends on education about AIDS, on changes in sexual practices, and
on changing societal attitudes towards people with AIDS. Professionals
in the community, including pharmacists, should take every
opportunity to increase levels of knowledge about AIDS in schools, local
organisations and in those seeking contraceptive advice.

Counselling

Once any form of HIV-related illness is diagnosed counselling is similar
to that for cancer, except that patients are younger and more prone to
feelings of guilt and despair. Suicide attempts are not uncommon
shortly after patients are informed of sero-positivity although these are
less marked later in the disease, when a more positive 'I will beat this'
attitude often occurs. Initially, people with positive HIV tests show

shock and disbelief which rapidly gives way to fear and anxiety about the future. It will be necessary to explore the individual's doubts and worries which may concern the course, treatment and outcome of the illness, such as rejection by society or sexual partners, or about the loss of autonomy and self-image. General aspects of communication with terminally ill patients is covered in Chapter 5.

Antiviral therapy

At present, only one drug is licensed for direct treatment of HIV infection. Zidovudine (Retrovir R), formerly Azidothymidine (AZT), acts by mimicking thymidine, thereby inhibiting the insertion of viral RNA in the host cell nucleus. Thymidine is required in the process by which reverse transcriptase encodes the RNA of HIV into the host lymphocyte. Early treatment of the asymptomatic HIV positive patient, whose T4 is greater than 500 per cmm, with zidovudine has been shown to delay the development of immunosuppression. There is some evidence that AZT reduces mortality and morbidity in people with AIDS who have already suffered pneumocystis carinii pneumonia or other severe opportunistic infections.

Zidovudine is toxic and expensive and should only be prescribed by those experienced in its use.

Recent suggestions have been made regarding the treatment of AIDS patients with a combination of zidovudine and acyclovir. This development should be watched with interest. (The present licensed indications for acyclovir are herpes simplex and varicella-zoster).

A large number of other drugs are under development by the pharmaceutical industry. A few of these have reached the controlled clinical trial stage. All are toxic and none offers any more than hope of delay of the development of immunosuppression. A drug-induced cure does not seem possible at this stage. Likewise, a curative vaccine is extremely unlikely, although a preventive vaccine may be developed in time.

Unfortunately, a large number of quack remedies are being promoted. Those which have been scientifically studied have been proved totally ineffective. Patients should be discouraged from trying such remedies, particularly when this means they are avoiding professional medical care.

Symptom control

The majority of patients with HIV-related illness are ambulant and as such are likely to be looked after in the community. Thus as the

Box 8.2: Common symptoms in AIDS and their cause

System	Symptoms	Cause				
		VIRUSES	BACTERIA	PROTOZOA	FUNGI	
RESPIRATORY	cough dyspnoea	Cytomegalovirus Herpes simplex	Mycobacteria pneumococcus H. influenzae	Pneumocystis carinii	Cryptoccocus	
GASTRO- INTESTINAL	dysphagia high volume diarrhoea	Cytomegalovirus Herpes simplex	Mycobacteria Salmonella	Cryptosporidium Isospora belli Microsporidia	Candida	
CENTRAL NERVOUS	meningitic encephalitic dementia	Cytomegalovirus Herpes simplex Papovavirus	Mycobacteria	Toxoplasma	Aspergillus Cryptoccocus Candida	
SKIN	all skin conditions are worse	Herpes simplex	Staphylococci		Candida Tinea	
GENERAL	fever weight loss malaise	consider all types of infection				

epidemic increases there is likely to be a heavy burden on general practitioners, nurses and other health care staff including pharmacists. Symptom control depends on cause which is usually due to opportunistic infections which are listed in Box 8.2.

Respiratory symptoms

Respiratory symptoms are commonly caused by chest infections which may be viral, bacterial, protozoan or fungal. Respiratory symptoms may also be caused by pulmonary lesions of Kaposi's sarcoma. Bacterial infection should be treated with the appropriate antibiotic. Infections with atypical forms of Mycobacteria respond to normal anti-tuberculous treatment. Pneumonia due to pneumocystis carinii is treated orally with co-trimoxazole 20 mg/Kg per day. As an alternative, pentamidine 4 mg/ Kg per day may be used by intravenous infusion, or by inhalation of nebulised solution. Pentamidine is an alternative to co-trimoxazole for patients with a history of adverse reactions to co-trimoxazole.

Gastrointestinal symptoms

Gastrointestinal symptoms are very common with high volume diarrhoea due to protozoan disease: cryptosporidiosis, Isospora or microsporidia. Bacterial causes include mycobacteria, salmonella and campylobacter. Where possible the cause should be identified and treated, but often this is not possible. No reliably effective treatment exists for cryptosporidiosis. Parisitological and symptomatic cure of Isospora has been reported with pyrimethamine-sulphadiazine, trimethoprim, sulphamethoxazole, and furazolidone. Symptomatic treatment involves fluid replacement and codeine phosphate or loperamide.

Mouth problems are extremely common, especially caries, gingivitis and ulceration of the fauces. Infection may be aphthous, herpetic, fungal or bacterial. Candida is especially common and its presence in the mouth of a young man is highly suggestive of HIV infection unless he is using betamethasone aerosols for asthma. Tongue lesions are common and hairy leukoplakia, seen as white flat warty projections on the lateral side of the tongue, is unique to those infected with HIV (*see* Appendix D for treatment of oral problems).

Dysphagia is common and often due to severe oesophageal candida which may be slow to respond to nystatin and may require aggressive treatment with amphotericin or ketoconazole.

Central nervous system

As many as 75% of people with AIDS show postmortem evidence of disease of the central nervous system but only some 10% have neurological symptoms which may be caused by the virus itself, either because of opportunistic infection or because of tumours. About a third of patients with AIDS develop a subacute encephalitis caused by HIV. In mild cases there may be forgetfulness and loss of concentration with lethargy and loss of motor function. HIV encephalopathy may coexist with opportunistic infection or tumours.

Meningitis may occur in AIDS due to Cryptococcus neoformans. It is less florid in its symptomatology than acute bacterial meningitis but may resemble tuberculous meningitis. It presents with malaise and fever, headache with nausea and vomiting and there may be photophobia and neck stiffness. Space occupying lesions may be caused by opportunistic infection such as toxoplasmosis, or abscesses caused by mycobacteria or candida. Other neurological manifestations of AIDS occur as progressive multifocal leucoencephalopathy (a form of demyelinating disease, resembling multiple sclerosis). Treatment of neurological disease depends on treating the opportunistic infection where possible. Systemic fungal infection may respond to amphotericin, atypical mycobacteria respond to standard anti-tuberculous therapy and toxoplasmosis requires long-term treatment with sulphonamides, clindamycin and pyrimethamine.

Skin

Almost all skin conditions become more florid in the presence of immunosuppression. All infective skin conditions, viral, bacterial or fungal are particularly severe and require energetic treatment. Herpes simplex (particularly anal or genital) and herpes zoster are extremely severe in AIDS patients. Aggressive treatment with acyclovir is necessary.

Tumours

The most common tumour is a sarcoma which was originally described by Kaposi in 1872 and which has become much more common since the beginning of the AIDS epidemic. Individual lesions may occur anywhere but are most commonly seen in the skin or mouth. They are multifocal and pigmented, often purplish or brown and arise from vascular endothelium. Starting as a tiny skin blemish, they rapidly develop and may be widespread. Other malignant tumours include lymphoma and some forms of squamous cell cancer.

General

HIV-related conditions produce many non-specific general symptoms such as sweating, malaise, weakness, lethargy, myalgia, lymphadenopathy and extreme weight loss. These will require symptomatic treatment and treatment of underlying anxiety or depression. Principles of palliative care outlined in Chapter 3 apply equally to AIDS/HIV patients.

Control of infection

HIV is extremely fragile and of low infectivity unless there is blood-to-blood or semen-to-blood contact. (Transmission may occur vertically across the placenta or, possibly during breast-feeding.) This means that extreme care must be taken when handling potentially infected blood or tissue during surgery, venesection or in the laboratory. Blood suspected of being infected with HIV should be sent to the laboratory with full biohazard precautions. Accidental spillage of blood should be flooded with hypochlorite solutions containing 10,000 ppm of available chlorine (1 in 10 household bleach) and clothing contaminated with blood or semen should be autoclaved.

Conclusion

AIDS concerns everyone. However responsibility falls heaviest on those professionals who have daily contact with patients and to whom the man in the street turns for health advice. The community pharmacist may be the most accessible and easily approached.

The principles of palliative care outlined in this book apply equally to AIDS/HIV patients. Members of the public suffering from advanced cancer, motor neurone disease, AIDS or other terminal conditions will benefit from enlightened professional attitudes and real understanding of their special needs. Community pharmacists are in a position to deliver comprehensive pharmaceutical care to patients in the terminal stages of their illness.

Further reading

Adler, M.W. (Ed) 1988. *ABC of AIDS*. Br Med J, London
Anonymous. 1990. *Approaches to AIDS treatment. Chemist & Druggist* **234**: 984–6
Anonymous. 1991. Picking up the Strands of AIDS Research *Chemist & Druggist* **236**: 951

Chin, J. 1990. Current and Future Dimensions of the HIV/AIDS Pandemic in Women and Children. *The Lancet* **336**: 221–4

Clarbour, J. 1988. Update on the Treatment of AIDS and HIV disease. *Pharm J* **241**: 691–2

Department of Health, 1991. *On the State of the Public Health for the Year 1990.* 109–121. HMSO, London

Erskine, D. 1989. Update on the Drug Treatment of HIV. *Pharm J* **243**: 712–3

Erskine, D. 1991. Current Usage of Zidovudine. *Pharm J* **247**: 729–30

Harris, J.R.W. & Forster, S.M. 1991. *Sexually Transmitted Diseases and AIDS.* Churchill Livingstone, London

Health Education Authority, 1991. *AIDS Dialogue No. 10*

Hull, F.M. 1990. Unpublished Report to 'Help the Hospices' following Fellowship at Memorial Sloan Kettering Cancer Centre, New York

Hull, F.M. 1990. In: *Treatment and Prognosis in General Practice.* pp 324–326 (eds Drury, M. & Hobbs, R.) Heinemann Medical Books, Oxford

Knight, S. 1990. Developments in the Drug Treatment of AIDS. *Pharm J* **245**: 724–5

Temple, D.J. 1987. AIDS: Facts for Pharmacists. *Pharm J* **239**: 537–41

Temple, D.J. 1988. Epidemiology of AIDS. *Pharm J* **241**: 690–1

Temple, D.J. 1989. Why We Need a Second 'World AIDS Day'. *Pharm J* **243**: 710–11.

Temple, D.J. 1990. Update on AIDS Epidemiology. *Pharm J* **245**: 752–3

Temple, D.J. & Westwood, N. (Eds) 1988. *AIDS Now: Some questions answered.* Leicester Polytechnic

Appendix A: Useful Organisations

1   Cancer Relief Macmillan Fund

The Fund was founded in 1911 to bring care and support to cancer patients. Today, as a national charity, the role of the Fund is to help improve the lives of people with cancer, at any stage in their illness and in any setting including: their own home, the hospital or the specialised cancer unit. The Macmillan nurses are a vital part of this.

Macmillan nurses are specially trained to give supportive care to people with cancer, and their help extends to the whole family. They cover a wide spectrum of cancer care, working with patients at any point in their illness.

There are four kinds of Macmillan nurse. Currently, most are based in the community, caring for patients at home; a growing number work in hospitals. There are also Macmillan breast care nurses to support women with breast cancer; and Macmillan paediatric nurses, caring for children with cancer and their families. Whether in the community or in a hospital setting, Macmillan nurses work closely with doctors, nurses and other health care workers, sharing their expertise in pain and symptom control and in emotional counselling. Their role is that of a specialist offering advice, information and support to patients and their carers, and to their colleagues. Macmillan nurses have an important part to play in coordinating care, and their overall aim is to ensure that each patient receives the best possible care. Their knowledge and experience of cancer means that Macmillan nurses have an important role to play in improving the standard of care cancer patients receive.

All Macmillan nurses are Registered General Nurses and, if working in the community, must be qualified and experienced District Nurses or Health Visitors.

Funding for Macmillan nurses is provided by the Cancer Relief Macmillan Fund, usually for the first three years, and includes the cost of specialist training. After that time, financial responsibility is taken over by the Health Authority. Macmillan nurses work in teams of two or more in community services within the NHS, or in NHS hospital-based teams. A smaller number are attached to independent hospices. Wherever they are based, Macmillan nurses are available to cancer patients free of charge as part of the National Health Service. Requests for a Macmillan nurse should be made via the patient's GP, district nurse, consultant or ward sister.

Cancer Relief Macmillan Fund's Patient Grants Department provides financial help towards the cost of a wide range of goods and services for people with cancer on a low income. Grants are available where the DSS, local authorities and the NHS are unable to meet the needs of people with cancer. Grants are made for heating bills, treatment and visiting fares, domestic appliances and many other items. A nurse or social worker will apply on a patient's behalf since direct applications are not possible.

CancerLink provides support, information and publications for people affected by cancer, at the time of diagnosis, treatment, if the cancer comes back or if they wish to use the experience they have had to support others.

The Breast Care and Mastectomy Association provides emotional support and practical information for women who have, or fear they may have, breast cancer. There are over 700 volunteer helpers throughout the country, all of whom have had breast surgery and will offer individual support.

2   Marie Curie Cancer Care (Marie Curie Memorial Foundation)

The Marie Curie Memorial Foundation is a comprehensive cancer charity, covering all the following fields: residential homes, community nursing, welfare, information and advice, research, plus education and training.

The Foundation has 11 residential Marie Curie Homes providing accommodation and skilled nursing care for cancer patients in the following categories:

- Those requiring rehabilitation and/or continuing care.
- Short-term admissions for home-based patients in order to provide relatives with a rest period or to stabilise symptom/pain control regimes.
- Patients discharged from hospital requiring convalescence or stabilisation of symptom/pain control regimes prior to their return home.
- Patients undergoing outpatient treatment at regional centres where daily travel from home is difficult.

Applications for residential care are made to the matron concerned who can advise on admission procedures. Priority of admission is based solely on medical and/or social need. The Foundation is a non-sectarian organisation offering help to all in need.

In most areas of the United Kingdom the Foundation is able to provide nursing care for patients in their own homes through the Marie Curie Nursing Service. The main demand is for night nursing to enable those caring for a loved one at home to obtain adequate rest. This service, which provides 4,000 Marie Curie nurses nationwide, is administered on the Foundation's behalf at local level by NHS Health Authorities. There is no charge for the service, which is funded by the Foundation with Health Authority assistance in some areas.

In conjunction with the Foundation's home nursing, funds are available locally to provide, without administrative delay, urgent necessities in kind until such time as statutory or other sources can meet the need. Examples of items provided include extra bed linen, liquidisers, electric fans and other items of benefit to home-based cancer patients.

The Foundation's Information and Advisory Service operates in association with BACUP (British Association of Cancer United Patients), which offers information and emotional support to cancer patients and their relatives and friends through a team of Cancer Information Service Officers.

The Institute of Oncology aims to improve the care and treatment of cancer patients through courses for doctors and nurses, and to bring about a better understanding among the public of the nature, prevention and treatment of cancer.

The Marie Curie Research Institute in Surrey is developing as an important site for international cancer research and a valuable meeting centre for oncologists from around the world. The Institute carries out significant and vital research which is applied to specific human cancer problems.

3   Palliative care for the terminally ill – the contribution of the Sue Ryder Foundation

In the mid-1970s the Foundation opened a home at Oxenhope in West Yorkshire for the care of cancer patients with terminal illness. The financing of the home was aided by the help of the local medical practice, who undertook the day to day care of the patients and prescribing was arranged by the registration of the patients as temporary residents. From this beginning the Foundation has now expanded its interest in care of the terminally ill to include over 200 beds in England and Scotland.

The expansion of the care for the terminally ill patients was associated with the general increase in the hospice movement throughout Great Britain, mainly for the care of cancer patients. Expansion of the hospice movement was aided by many surveys examining the need, including that in the Oxford region in 1968. These surveys confirmed that many patients were dying at home and in hospital in highly unsatisfactory conditions. It was estimated that about 25 beds would be required per half a million of the population and of necessity, many of these patients would be in the older age groups as there is a dramatic increase in the incidence of cancer after the fifth decade in life. Since many patients were elderly, the ability to give terminal care at home was correspondingly much more difficult. Against this it was also appreciated that those in the younger age groups might be the breadwinners who were unable to work and this would also produce serious problems, both medical and social, requiring far more help than was available at the time.

The Sue Ryder Foundation played an important part in the development of the hospice movement, although Lady Ryder has always been very keen to describe her hospices as 'homes', thereby distinguishing them from the hospital atmosphere with an unnecessary and inappropriate clinical ambience. However, the homes have, in line with other similar institutions, kept up a very high standard of nursing care for the terminally ill. It has been appreciated that palliative care of the terminally ill is a nursing orientated speciality and attempts, as in the past, to care for these patients with an unsatisfactory nursing cover are worse than useless. It is generally agreed that approximately 1.5 nurses per patient are required in the establishment of a hospice. The work not only involves careful and regular medication for pain and other symptoms, but also much time is spent in talking to patients and to their relatives.

The Foundation's homes provide inpatient care for patients with a wide range of disabilities, including ten homes specifically for the continuing care of patients with advanced malignant cancer. Domiciliary care teams and bereavement counsellors also operate from some homes.

The Sue Ryder Foundation
Founder: Lady Ryder of Warsaw CMG OBE

4   The Association of Hospice Social Workers (AHSW)

The role of the social worker

Social work has an important complementary role in terminal care. The medical social worker's task has been traditionally to help families with social, emotional or practical problems. An individual social worker may be allocated to the primary team caring for a patient. An alternative can be liaison with a hospital social worker who has a special interest in the care of the terminally ill. A number of support care teams have a social worker specifically attached.

As a non-medical person, the social worker is often in a position to stand back from the medical and nursing aspects of patient care and can act as a bridge between patients, families and staff. The patient and the family can be helped to identify important questions which can then be directed to the appropriate staff members. The social worker also has a practical input to make in such issues as discharge planning and locating appropriate financial and other resources in the community.

The Association of Hospice Social Workers

The Association of Hospice Social Workers (AHSW) is a professional association of social workers working in hospices, hospice home care teams and hospice home care teams in hospitals, throughout the United Kingdom and Ireland.

Social workers in hospice care offer:

- skilled counselling to patients and families;
- family casework/therapy;
- group work;
- research;
- teaching to multidisciplinary groups;
- management, training and supervision of bereavement support services;
- advocacy and advice on welfare rights.

The AHSW has links with numerous organisations associated with palliative care and bereavement.

Attendance allowance in terminal illness

The AHSW has been instrumental in achieving revision of criteria for qualification for Attendance Allowance – an important extra financial benefit to help families care for people with a terminal illness at home.

Details of this allowance are contained in the Attendance Allowance Claim Pack D52 (1990), available from Department of Social Security offices.

The allowance is a weekly benefit for people who need help because of their illness or disability. The new 'special rules' make it easier for people with a terminal illness to obtain an allowance. Applicants do not have to wait for six months before an allowance can be paid, as in the past; and claims are dealt with swiftly by the inclusion of a doctor's report (D51500 Report) on the claimant's medical condition. In Social Security law, 'terminally ill' means that a person has a progressive disease and has a reasonable expectation of life of six months or less.

The AHSW is keen for all professionals involved in terminal care in the community to be aware of the attendance allowance and the special rules for terminally ill patients.

5   Motor Neurone Disease Association (MNDA)

The Association was registered as a charity in 1979 and exists to provide help, advice, information and support to people coping with Motor Neurone Disease (MND). Three people die each day from MND and 6,000 people in Britain cope with its effects.

MNDA National Office can provide information leaflets (requests exceed 300 per month) to people with MND, health care professionals, carers and friends. One useful leaflet written with professionals in mind is: *Symptom Control in Motor Neurone Disease*.

A network of 14 Regional Care Advisers exists. Advisers are involved in visiting to give support and advice face to face, and in liaising with health care professionals. This ensures families receive available statutory services. Advisers can be involved in the Association's national educational activities.

MNDA's equipment loan service is a partnership between statutory services, the local branch, the National Office and the patient/carer team in the home. Chairs, mattresses, light writers and voice synthesisers can give comfort and independence and each can contribute to improved quality of life. General support is provided through a counselling service, including a telephone helpline. The service aims to offer support whenever someone needs it.

Applied research is undertaken which should result in direct benefit to the quality of life for people with MND. Current projects include: making and adapting aids for independent living; research into the fields of mobility and communication; partnership with the MONITOR Trust in the National Patient Register.

The network of 70 MNDA branches gives care and support through volunteer services. Branches also exist to raise awareness of MND in their area and to raise money for both patient care and research.

6   The Lisa Sainsbury Foundation

Set up with charitable status in 1984, and after a period for initial research, the Foundation became operational in October 1985. The policy of the Foundation is to:

- encourage the education and training of health care professionals working with dying patients and their families;
- support staff working with dying people and their families and friends;
- encourage and develop the links between the ideals and practice of hospice care and the care of people dying at home or in hospital settings.

The work of the Foundation is carried out in the following ways:

- *Workshops*. Requests for workshops are received from all parts of the United Kingdom and it is usual to arrange over 250 each year. Workshops can be tailored to meet the precise needs of a group, which may be multidisciplinary. The topics covered may include talking with patients and relatives, communication, counselling skills, bereavement and loss.
- *Loans*. (i) Syringe drivers – these are lent on request to meet the needs of a specific patient. (ii) Portable cassette players – some patients find it helpful to listen to music or the spoken word and these can be lent on the same basis as syringe drivers.
- *Books*. Books available in the Lisa Sainsbury Foundation series include:

1	Caring for Dying People of Different Faiths	Rabbi Julia Neuberger
2	Missed Beginnings – Death Before Life has been Established	June Jolly
3	Pain Control	Jane Latham
4	Communicating with Dying People and their Relatives	Jean Lugton
5	Radiotherapy	Susan Holmes
6	Loss and Bereavement	Bridget Cook & Shelagh Phillips

- *Information*. A newsletter, book bibliography, reading lists and other information are all available on request.

7 The Hospice Information Service

The Hospice Information Service was founded in 1977 by St Christopher's Hospice in response to a growing number of enquiries relating to the work of hospices. Originally funded solely from the general income of St Christopher's Hospice, the service now also receives generous financial support from the Cancer Relief Macmillan Fund which has enabled extra staffing and development.

The Hospice Information Service is a national resource: it provides an information exchange and link for those working in hospices, or with terminally ill patients and families, as well as for members of the public. The main functions of the service are:

- provision of information on the nature and location of hospices both in the United Kingdom and overseas;
- annual publication of a Directory of Hospices in the United Kingdom and Ireland;
- collection of fact sheets on various aspects of planning, development and management of services;
- a regular newsletter, *The Bulletin*, of interest to those working in hospice;
- the compilation of a database to obtain a national picture of hospice services. Areas covered will reflect questions most commonly asked and may be of particular interest to groups setting up new hospice services.

Enquiries are welcomed and should be sent to:

Hospice Information Service
St Christopher's Hospice
51–59 Lawrie Park Road
Sydenham
London SE26 6DZ
Tel: 081-778 9252 ext 262/3
Fax: 081-659 8680

Appendix B: Useful Addresses

This appendix comprises a selection of organisations providing help and advice to health care professionals, patients and their families.

AIDS – The Terrence Higgins Trust Ltd
53–54 Gray's Inn Road
London WC1X 8JU
Tel: 071-831 0330

ALZHEIMER'S DISEASE SOCIETY
158–160 Balham High Road
London SW12 9BN
Tel: 081-675 6557

ASSOCIATION OF HOSPICE SOCIAL WORKERS
Hospice at Home
Michael Tetley Hall
Sandhurst Road
Tunbridge Wells TN2 3JS
Tel: 0892-544877

BACUP (British Association of Cancer United Patients)
121/123 Charterhouse Street
London EC1M 6AA
Tel: 071-608 1661

CRUSE – Bereavement Care
Cruse House
126 Sheen Road
Richmond
Surrey TW9 1UR
Tel: 081-940 4818

CANCER RELIEF MACMILLAN FUND
15/19 Britten Street
London SW3 3TZ
Tel: 071-351 7811

CANCERLINK
17 Britannia Street
London WC1X 8JN
Tel: 071-833 2451
and
9 Castle Terrace
Edinburgh EH1 2DP
Tel: 031-228 5557

CARERS NATIONAL ASSOCIATION
29 Chilworth Mews
London W2 3RG
Tel: 071-724 7776
and
11 Queen's Crescent
Glasgow G4 9AS
Tel: 041-333 9495

DISABLED LIVING FOUNDATION
380 Harrow Road
London W9 2HU
Tel: 071-289 8320

HALLEY STEWART LIBRARY
St Christopher's Hospice
51 Lawrie Park Road
Sydenham
London SE26 6DZ
Tel: 081-778 9252

HELP THE AGED
St James Walk
London EC1R 0BE
Tel: 071-253 0253

HELP THE HOSPICES
34–44 Britannia Street
London WC1X 9JG
Tel: 071-278 5668

HOSPICE INFORMATION SERVICE
St Christopher's Hospice
51 Lawrie Park Road
Sydenham
London SE26 6DZ
Tel: 081-778 9252

LISA SAINSBURY FOUNDATION
8–10 Crown Hill
Croydon
Surrey CR0 1RY
Tel: 081-686 8808

MARIE CURIE CANCER CARE
Head Office
28 Belgrave Square
London SW1X 8QG
Tel: 071-235 3325
and
Scottish Office
21 Rutland Square
Edinburgh EH1 2HA
Tel: 031-229 8332

MOTOR NEURONE DISEASE ASSOCIATION
P.O. Box 246
Northampton NN1 2PR
Tel: 0604-250505 or 22269

SUE RYDER FOUNDATION
Sue Ryder Home
Cavendish
Sudbury
Suffolk CO10 8AY
Tel: 0787-280252

Appendix C: Example of Body Chart for Pain Assessment

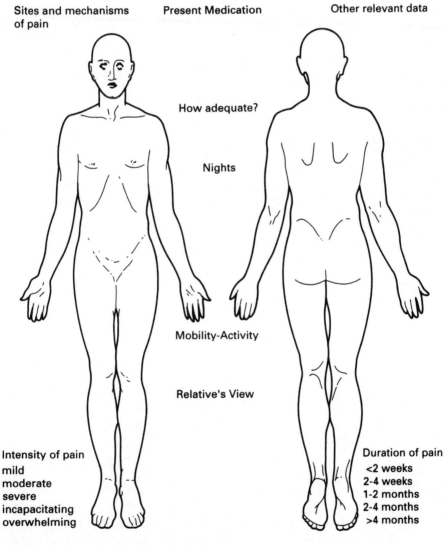

Sites and mechanisms of pain

Present Medication

Other relevant data

How adequate?

Nights

Mobility-Activity

Relative's View

Intensity of pain
mild
moderate
severe
incapacitating
overwhelming

Duration of pain
<2 weeks
2-4 weeks
1-2 months
2-4 months
>4 months

Reproduced from: Twycross R.G. and Lack S.A. (1990). *Therapeutics in Terminal Cancer*. Churchill Livingstone, London

The chart is usually filled in by the doctor, with the help of the patient. Areas where pain is felt are shaded in, together with characteristics of the pain itself (constant, intermittent, dull, aching, shooting, gnawing), and whether the pain is worse standing, sitting or on movement – together with any exacerbating or relieving factors such as alcohol or drugs.

Appendix D: Further Aspects of Palliative Care (see also Chapter 3)

1 Sore mouth – oral problems

Problem	Causes	Features	Treatment
Dry mouth	Dehydration, Phenothiazines tricyclics, hyoscine etc	Dry tongue, thick saliva, difficulty speaking	Oral hydration if possible. Sucking: crushed ice, butter, frozen tonic water. Chewing: pineapple chunks. Change drugs: e.g. amitriptyline to mianserin, prochlorperazine to haloperidol
Coated tongue	Debility, poor oral hygiene, dehydration, candida	white/brown or black tongue, reduced taste, halitosis	Cleansing: 2% sodium bicarb, or 6% hydrogen peroxide. Dissolving: 1 g effervescent ascorbic acid on tongue. Brushing: gently with toothbrush. Chewing: pineapple chunks
Candidiasis (Thrush)	Debility, cross-infection, poor oral hygiene	1 White adherent patches, coated tongue dryness 2 Redness, soreness or dryness only 3 Chelitis 4 Ulceration only	Nystatin 1 ml 4 hourly. Ketoconazole 200 mg mane (1 tab or 10 ml susp) for 1 week. Soak dentures daily in weak Milton – do not use denture solutions. Mouthwash: povidone-iodine (Betadine)

Problem	Causes	Features	Treatment
Ulceration	Apthous ulcers Radiotherapy Chemotherapy Dentures Poor dental hygiene	White depressions in mucosa with surrounding inflammation. Painful.	Tetracycline syrup 10 ml (250 mg) mouthwash for 2 m then swallowed. Triamcinolone in Orabase Betamethasone 1 mg dissolved in water as a mouthwash
	Herpes simplex Herpes zoster	Pale vesicles with surrounding redness. Painful. Unilateral in herpes zoster	Treat as for painful mouth. Consider: acyclovir 200 mg 4 h for 5 days
Painful mouth	Ulceration Candidiasis Poor oral hygiene Oral cancer Oral sepsis	Soreness talking, eating and swallowing	Benzydamine (Difflam) as mouthwash 1– 2 hourly. Choline salicylate (Bonjela, Teejel) to local lesions. Consider: antibiotics if sepsis, local anaesthetics prior to cleaning mouth
Halitosis	Oral cancer + sepsis Lung cancer + sepsis Bowel obstruction	Pus in mouth, debris, infected sputum, faeculant vomiting, poor oral hygiene	Povidone-iodine (Betadine) mouthwash. Consider: antibiotics if sepsis present

Reproduced: from C.F.B. Regnard and A. Davies, *A Guide to Symptom Relief in Advanced Cancer*. Manchester, Haigh and Hochland 1986.

2 Urinary incontinence

Cause	First line	Second line	Consider
Post-prostatectomy	Propantheline (Pro-Banthine) 15 mg before meals + 30 mg nocte (up to 90 mg daily)	Imipramine 50–100 mg nocte	Condom, urethral catheter or bag. Desmopressin nasally may help
Stress incontinence	Ring pessary	Ephedrine 30 mg bd. last dose no later than 6 p.m.	Absorbant pads, tampons, surgery
Urge incontinence ('unstable bladder')	Propantheline (Pro-Banthine) 15 mg before meals + 30 mg nocte (up to 90 mg daily)	Imipramine 50–100 mg nocte	NSAID (e.g. flurbiprofen, pads, condom, urethral catheter or bag
Neuropathic bladder -spastic	Large capacity: manual stimulation to void, small capacity: intermittent catheterisation	Permanent condom, urethral catheter or bag	Desmopressin nocte may help
-flaccid	Regular voiding	Intermittent Catheterisation	
By-passing catheter	Exclude infection or bladder spasm	Halve balloon volume	Change to smaller size catheter
Vesico-vaginal fistula	Absorbant pads or tampons	Desmopressin nocte may help	

Reproduced from: C.F.B. Regnard and A. Davies, *A Guide to Symptom Relief in Advanced Cancer*. Manchester, Haigh and Hochland, 1986.

Appendix E: Bereavement

The death of someone close has a profound effect, even when the relationship has been difficult or ambivalent. Often the initial reaction is one of numbness, which can be accompanied by shock and disbelief. These feelings can act as a defence as the bereaved person tries to deal with the reality of death. As the reality of the situation begins to be absorbed, the grief becomes more prominent.

With time the feelings of numbness fade, while the pain of grieving increases. This stage can include searching for the dead person, increased feelings of helplessness and anxiety and sometimes anger. The latter may be expressed at the dead person or at the carers such as professional staff.

The bereaved will often go over the events surrounding the death trying to make sense of what has happened. The events preceding and surrounding the time of death can affect these early stages of grief. Thus good palliative care of the dying person and counselling of the family around the time of death can ease bereavement.

The various aspects of grief are shown in Box E.1.

With time there is a gradual lessening of the feelings of acute grief. The bereaved may have become socially isolated as they became disinterested in everything around them. This may continue for several months followed by a gradual acceptance of the loss.

The stages of loss and bereavement outlined above are not clear cut. However, with time, most bereaved people are able to live fully again, although altered by the experience of the loss.

Abnormal grief reactions may occur and in these circumstances expert help from a bereavement counsellor psychiatrist may be necessary. Delayed, inhibited or chronic grief are forms of abnormal grief, which can be exacerbated by the absence of a supportive social network. Special losses such as suicide, a sudden death, or even a death from AIDS can bring increased difficulties for the bereaved.

Although the majority of people die in hospital, most of the grieving will take place at home. The primary health care team has the

---

Box E.1: Manifestations of normal grief

Feelings	*Physical sensations*
Sadness	Hollowness in stomach
Anger	Tightness in chest or throat
Guilt	Over sensitivity to noise
Anxiety	Sense of depersonalisation
Loneliness	Breathlessness
Helplessness	Weakness
Shock	Lack of energy
Yearning	Dry mouth
Emancipation	
Relief	
Numbness	

Thoughts	*Behaviour*
Disbelief	Sleep disturbance
Confusion	Appetite disturbance
Preoccupation	Social withdrawal
Sense of presence	Dreams of deceased
Hallucinations	Avoiding reminders of deceased
	Searching and calling out
	Sighing
	Restless over-activity
	Crying
	Visiting places to remind survivor of deceased
	Treasuring deceased's objects

Adapted from: Worden, J.W. 1983. *Grief Counselling and Grief Therapy*. Tavistock Publications, London

---

opportunity to help at this time. Pharmacists may be asked for advice on poor appetite or sleeplessness while the bereavement underlying these complaints may need tackling. Good listening is often more important than medication, as anxiolytics or sedatives can mask the feelings which eventually need to be expressed. As a general rule, drugs should be prescribed sparingly in the treatment of the bereaved.

Counselling has been shown to be successful in reducing the morbidity of bereavement. Most hospices provide a volunteer counselling service for the families of their patients. CRUSE Bereavement Care is a national organisation for the bereaved, while local clergy or church groups may also be able to provide both practical and emotional support.

When appropriate, pharmacists can encourage people to seek help through counselling from these support facilities. Pharmacists who have been involved in the care preceding a death may well have the opportunity to help directly or indirectly during the time of bereavement.

Further reading

Parkes, C.M. 1986. *Bereavement: studies of grief in adult life*. Penguin, Harmondsworth

1989. *Someone Special has Died*. St Christopher's Hospice, Department of Social Work

Cook B. & Phillips, S. 1988. *Loss and Bereavement*. Austen Cornish Publishers Ltd and the Lisa Sainsbury Foundation

Appendix F: Home Chemotherapy Working Party Report: Summary of Recommendations

1   That community pharmacists become more involved in the treatment of cancer patients in the community, particularly those being treated by continuous infusion.

2   That community pharmacists play a greater role in providing advice to general medical practitioners, nurses and patients on cancer chemotherapy.

3   That community pharmacists play a greater role in the supply of medications for treating the terminally ill.

4   That community pharmacists should be given advance notice of a patient's discharge from hospital to avoid last minute requests for Controlled Drugs which might not be in stock.

5   That greater liaison should take place between community pharmacists and their hospital colleagues to encourage the exchange of information on patients.

6   That community pharmacists should supply equipment such as syringe drivers for cancer chemotherapy and pumps for nasogastric feeds, the supply of this equipment being analogous to the pharmacist's present responsibilities for oxygen equipment.

7   That more frequent contacts should take place between community pharmacists and specialist nurses in the areas of cancer chemotherapy, diabetic therapy and terminal care.

8   That the British Diabetic Association be asked to advise its members of the need to inform community pharmacists, when seeking advice or presenting any prescriptions, that they are diabetic.

9   That community pharmacies should supply equipment such as blood glucose meters.

10 That educational material be provided for community pharmacists in the areas of cancer chemotherapy, *terminal care*, enteral nutrition and diabetic therapy.

Source: 1990. *The Pharmaceutical Journal*, **244**, 109

Appendix G: General Use of the Graseby Syringe Driver

Requirements:

- Prescription from doctor
- Syringe driver (MS26 for 24 hour delivery)
- Battery
- Syringe
- Butterfly cannula/sc catheter and extension set
- Transparent dressing i.e. Tegaderm, OpSite or Blenderm tape
- Antiseptic swab

Setting up the syringe driver

1 Full explanation of its purpose and how it works should be given to patients and carers.
2 Medication and sterile water drawn up to volume.
3 Butterfly needle/sc catheter and tubing connected to syringe. Primed with solution (approximately 0.5 ml).
4 Battery inserted and spare battery kept available.
5 Start/test button pressed: Machine will produce a soft whirring and indicator light will flash on/off.
6 Rate checked, set correctly on front of syringe driver. (Usually set to deliver contents of syringe in 24 hours).
7 Syringe fitted with infusion tubing and needle attached to syringe driver. Flange of syringe placed in slot provided and secured with rubber strap. Extra tape may be used to secure syringe to pump.
8 Plunger fitted. White release button pressed, then plunger assembly slid until it presses against syringe plunger. Pump now ready for use.

Inserting the cannula

1   Site chosen for the butterfly needle/sc catheter. The most useful sites are the upper chest, outer aspect of upper arm, abdomen and thighs (never in an oedematous area).
2   Needle inserted at 45 degrees subcutaneously.
3   Butterfly/sc catheter covered with transparent dressing. Small circle of tubing anchored to prevent 'pulling on butterfly'.
4   Clear plastic case placed into the holster and pump inserted into the case.

Notes
Site should be checked daily and changed if area is inflamed, painful or lumpy.

Light stops flashing when battery is low; pump will continue to operate for 24 hours after this. Battery lasts approximately six weeks.

Parenteral administration of opioid analgesics

A 24 hour dose of the diamorphine (an antiemetic may be added if necessary) is drawn into a syringe which is fitted into the Graseby syringe driver (MS 26) to which a cannula, with a butterfly needle/sc catheter, is attached. The setting is adjustable to deliver the contents of the syringe at a controlled rate, usually over 24 hours. The butterfly/sc catheter is inserted subcutaneously (usually in the suprascapular region), never into an oedematous region. Excellent and continuous pain control is achieved with this method and often with a smaller total dose of medication. The syringe is re-charged daily and it is wise to change the site of the needle/sc catheter every two or three days. Occasionally, local indurations develop at the needle site but these are nearly always caused by phenothiazines which have been added to the diamorphine as anti-emetics.

A useful formula when changing from oral morphine to administration of diamorphine via the syringe driver is to divide the daily dose of morphine by three. This gives the daily dose of diamorphine, i.e. if a patient is receiving 20 mg of oral morphine 4 hourly the daily dose is 120 mg divided by three = 40 mg. Therefore the dose of diamorphine in the syringe driver is 40 mg daily.

Reproduced from: Hanratty, J.F. 1989. *Palliative Care of the Terminally Ill*. Radcliffe Medical Press, Oxford

Drugs employed in syringe drivers (in a hospice or cancer hospital)

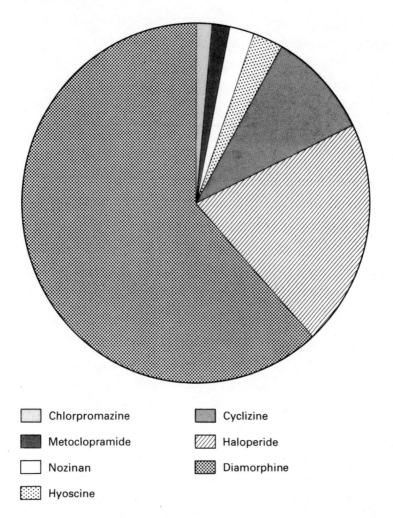

Chlorpromazine		Cyclizine	
Metoclopramide		Haloperide	
Nozinan		Diamorphine	
Hyoscine			

The most common analgesic used in the driver in terminal care in the United Kingdom is diamorphine (morphine in the United States).

Reproduced from: Twycross, R.G. (ed). 1989. *Edinburgh Symposium on Pain Control and Medical Education*. Royal Society of Medicine, London.

Appendix H: Courses, Videotapes and Journals

The Open University

The Department of Health and Social Welfare at the Open University is developing a new course and study pack on Death and Dying, funded by the Department of Health. The course will be produced in two formats to provide maximum flexibility of use:

- a multimedia study pack of learning materials; free-standing and available in both individual and group leader formats (approximate price £85 and £175 respectively);
- a 100-hour, quarter-credit course with tuition and assessment within the Diploma in Health and Social Welfare (approximate price £165).

Key themes: enabling dying people to feel respected and valued with emphasis on partnership rather than passivity.

Terminal care information folder

Published by the Royal College of General Practitioners (RCGP), editor Dr Colin Waine.

The Clinical and Research Division of the RCGP established a Terminal Care Working Party in 1988. The information folder was written by members of the Working Party, after having explored the issues involved in the delivery of high quality terminal care in general practice.

A useful home-study folder, price £15.00, covering:

- symptom control
- role of the hospice
- bereavement
- teaching terminal care – current provision of formal instruction.

English National Board of Nursing

Nurses intending to specialise in terminal care are able to undertake the English National Board:

- course 931 'The Continuing Care of the Dying Patient and the Family', a 30 day course;
- course 285 'Specialist Course in the Continuing Care of the Dying Patient and the Family', an 8 week course intended for those nurses who have completed course 931.

Diploma in Palliative Medicine

The University of Wales College of Medicine has established a course designed specifically for GPs and other experienced doctors who wish to gain expertise in the practical management of patients with non-curable and terminal illness, and aspects of cancer care. The one-year extra-mural diploma takes advantage of home and practice-based learning techniques. Most of the educational process is problem orientated, but linked to general scientific principles. Course materials are provided as audio teaching programmes, structured weekly reading, regular clinical exercises, plus clinical attachment. The course is organised into six modules.

The Cancer Relief Macmillan Fund provided financial support for the development of the course. The local Marie Curie Hospice is the base for three course weekends and is involved in the organisation of the course with the Department of General Practice.

Macmillan Palliation in Advanced Cancer (MacPac)

A computer and distance learning pack, funded by the Cancer Relief Macmillan Fund and developed by an interdisciplinary team based at the University of Glasgow and the Centre for Medical Education, Dundee University.

The MacPac Computer Challenge is a computer programme distributed by Napp Laboratories on behalf of CRMF. MacPac allows general practitioners to study case histories of different cancer patients and to try out various treatments for pain relief. The programme simulates the progress of the illness and reports on the effectiveness of the treatments chosen.

Palliative Care Distance Learning Programme

A series of eight audiotapes and review material, produced by Napp
Laboratories, primarily for nurses but made available to other primary
health care professionals. Subjects covered include:

- analgesic drugs in the management of cancer pain;
- the control of other symptoms in advanced cancer;
- communication in palliative care.

(Pharmacists interested in receiving the programme should contact
Napp Laboratories; the likely fee is £12.00).

Video tapes

Terminal cancer; approaches to pain management, 1989.
Rorer Pharmaceuticals*

Dying at home 1986.
Part 1 – the team approach (25 mins)
Part 2 – the management of cancer pain (30 mins)
Napp Laboratories*

The management of cancer pain.
Dr R.G. Twycross
Napp Laboratories*

Syringe drivers (9 minutes)
Department of Teaching Media
The General Hospital
Tremona Road
Southampton

Handling difficult questions (39 mins)
Dr Peter Maguire (hospital-based)
Tavistock Publications
11 New Fetter Lane
London EC4P 4EE

*available through the Audiovisual Loan Service of the Royal
Pharmaceutical Society.

Caring for your relative at home
Marie Curie Cancer Care
28 Belgrave Square
London SW1X 8QG

Living life to the full
Help the Hospices
34–44 Britannia Street
London WC1X 9JG

Journals

Palliative Medicine (quarterly). Edward Arnold

Geriatric Medicine (monthly). Findlay Publications Ltd

Journal of Pain and Symptom Management. Elsevier

Appendix I: Cancer Pain Relief and Palliative Care Report of a WHO Expert Committee

Recommendation to Member States

Implementation of the following recommendations, which could have a major impact on the quality of life of cancer patients, will require strong political motivation and leadership but can be undertaken without high expenditure.

1   Governments should establish national policies and programmes for cancer pain relief and palliative care.
2   Governments of Member States should ensure that cancer pain relief and palliative care programmes are incorporated into their existing health care systems: separate systems of care are neither necessary nor desirable.
3   Governments should ensure that health care workers (physicians, nurses, pharmacists, or other categories appropriate to local needs) are adequately trained in palliative care and the relief of cancer pain.
4   Governments should review their national health policies to ensure that equitable support is provided for programmes of palliative care in the home.
5   In the light of the financial, emotional, physical and social burdens carried by family members who are willing to care for cancer patients in the home, governments should consider establishing formal systems of recompense for the principal family care-givers.
6   Governments should recognise the singular importance of home care for patients with advanced cancer and should ensure that hospitals are able to offer appropriate back-up and support for home care.
7   Governments should ensure the availability of both opioid and non-opioid analgesics, particularly morphine for oral administration. Further, they should make realistic determinations of their opioid requirements and ensure that annual estimates submitted to the INCB reflect actual needs.

8   Governments should ensure that their drug legislation makes full provision for the following:

- regular review, with the aim of permitting importation, manufacture, prescribing, stocking, dispensing and administration of opioids for medical reasons;
- legally empowering physicians, nurses, pharmacists and, where necessary, other categories of health care worker, to prescribe, stock, dispense and administer opioids;

9   With pressure for the legalisation of euthanasia likely to increase, governments should make strenous efforts to keep fully informed of all developments in the fields of cancer pain relief, palliative care and management of terminal cancer.

WHO Expert Committee. 1990. *Cancer Pain Relief in Palliative Care*, Technical Report 804. WHO, Geneva.

Index

acceptance 13
Acquired Immune Deficiency
  Syndrome *see* AIDS
acute confusional state 40
acyclovir 95, 98
admixtures 56–7, 58
agonists 28
AIDS 90–1
  antiviral therapy 95
  cases in United Kingdom 91
  clinical aspects 93–4
  counselling in 94–5
  dementia in 40
  hospice policy towards 2
  palliative care 94
  spread of 92–3
  symptom control 95–9
AIDS-related complex 94
alcohol 45
alternative therapy 16
Alzheimer's Disease Society 109
ambulatory infusion devices 54–6,
  57, 73, 123–5
amitriptyline 32, 33
analgesia 27–30, 49–61
  in acute/chronic pain 26
analgesic ladder 28, 49–50
anger 12–13
antagonists 28, 34
anticholinergics 34, 37
antidepressants 32–3
  in insomnia 45
antiemetic drugs 34–6, 37
  admixtures 56–7

antihistamines 34, 37
anti-parkinson drugs 45
antiviral therapy, in AIDS 95
anxiety 13
apathy 19
apnoea 19
ARC 94
aspirin 28, 30, 31, 51
Association of Hospice Social
  Workers 104–6, 109
Ativan 20, 34, 37
atropine 34, 45
attendance allowance 105–6
AZT 95

BACUP 103, 109
barbiturates 45
bargaining 13
Baxter Multiday Infuser 54, 55, 56
benzodiazepines 45
bereavement 72, 119–21
beta-blockers 45
bisacodyl 40
body chart 27, 113–14
body position 72
brain death 19
Breast Care and Mastectomy
  Association 102
Brompton cocktail 53
buprenorphine 29
  availability 86
  control of 76
butyrophenones 34, 37

Cancer Relief Macmillan Fund 4,
    101–2, 110
    Patient Grants Department 102
CancerLink 102, 110
candida infection, in AIDS 97
cardiovascular system, in terminal
    cancer 18
Care of People with Terminal Illness,
    The 74
carers, caring for 14–15
Carers National Association 110
central nervous system
    action of opioid analgesics in 29–
        30
    in AIDS 96, 98
    in terminal cancer 18–19
Cheyne-Stokes breathing 19
chlormethiazole 44, 45
chlorpromazine 20, 44
chronic pain syndrome 29
cimetidine 45
co-analgesics 60
co-danthramer 40
co-danthrosate 40
Co-proxamol 28, 50, 51
co-trimoxazole 97
codeine 28, 51
    control of 76
    formulations 49–50
coma 19
Commonwealth Pharmaceutical
    Association 87
communication 11–12, 15, 70–2
    in confusion 43
community nursing services 5
community pharmacists 63–74, 123
compliance 65
confusion 40, 42–3
    drugs causing 45
    drugs used in management 44
constipation 39–40, 41
Continus 28, 52, 53
    control of 76
Convention on Psychotropic
    Substances 86
counselling, in AIDS 94–5
crisis points 46, 47

CRUSE 109, 120
cryptosporidiosis 97
Cyclimorph 76
cyclizine 34, 37
    admixtures with diamorphine 56–
        7
cytotoxic chemotherapy, role of
    community pharmacist 73, 123

danthron 40
day care 5
day centres 2
death
    acceptance of reality of 9
    approaching 19–20
    causes of 17–18
    patterns of 2–3
    signs of 20
death rattle 19–20, 38
Decadron 39
defence mechanisms, psychological
    12–13, 70
dementia
    in AIDS 94
    in terminal cancer 40
denial 12, 70
depression 13, 30, 32–3
dexamethasone 39
dextromoramide 28
    control of 76
dextropropoxyphene 28, 50, 51
diamorphine 28, 50–2
    admixtures 36, 56–7
    ambulatory infusion 54–6, 125
    control of 76
    formulations 50, 51–2
    parenteral formulation 53–4
diarrhoea
    in AIDS 97
    overflow 39
diazepam 38, 39, 44
    availability 86
Diconal 76
diflunisal 31
digoxin 45
dihydrocodeine 28, 51
dioctyl 40

diphenhydramine 34
dipipanone 76
Diploma in Palliative Medicine 130
Disabled Living Foundation 110
dispensing, controlled drugs 77
diuretics 45
Dolobid 31
domperidone 34, 37
dopamine antagonists 34, 37
dothiepin 33
droperidol 34
drug abuse, and AIDS 92
drugs
  administration route 58
  adverse effects 23
  appropriate prescription 23–4
  controlled
  delivery by third parties 79
  dispensing 77
  legislation 75
  levels of control 75–6
  prescriptions 76–7, 78
  recycling 80
  return for destruction 79–80
  security 79
  supply to hospices 80–1
  dosage 58
  interactions 23
  reasons for lack of effect 61
  shelf life 58
Dulcolax 40
Duragesic 88
dying
  patterns of 2–3
  physiology of 17–20
dynorphins 29
dysphagia, in AIDS 97
dyspnoea 36, 38–9

emesis 33–6
emotions, coping with 69–70
encephalitis, in AIDS 98
endorphins 29
English National Board of Nursing,
  courses 130
enkephalins 29
ethical issues 15–17

ethnic groups, ethical issues 17
Euhypnos 45
euthanasia 16–17
eyes, moisturising 19

faecal impaction 19, 36, 40
fear 30
flurbiprofen 28, 31
formulations 49
Fortral *see* pentazocine
fringe therapies 16
Froben 28, 31
frusemide 20
further education 129–32

gastrointestinal system
  in AIDS 96, 97
  in terminal cancer 18
gaze 72
general practitioners, and home care
  5–6
gesture 72
granisetron 36
Graseby MS26 Syringe Driver 54,
  55, 56, 125–7
grief, abnormal 119

hairy leukoplakia 97
Haldol 34, 37, 44, 56
Halley Stewart Library 110
haloperidol 34, 37, 44
  admixtures with diamorphine 56
Health Authorities 73–4
health professionals, risk of HIV
  infection 93
heart failure 18
Help The Aged 110
Help The Hospices 110
Heminevrin 44, 45
herpes simplex, in AIDS 98
herpes zoster, in AIDS 98
heterosexuals, and AIDS 93
history-taking 22
HIV 91
  control of infection 99
  spread of 92–3
HIV encephalopathy 98

home care services 2, 5, 13–14
  and the general practitioner 5–6
home care team 2
  interaction with community
    pharmacist 69
  need for continuity 14
homosexuals, and AIDS 92
hope 11, 12
hospice 4–5
  day 5
  supply of controlled drugs to 80–1
  teaching function 2
Hospice Information Service 107–8,
  111
hospice movement 1–2
hospice pharmacy, United States 88
  –9
Hospital Support Teams 3
hospitals
  admittance to 3–4
  communication with community
    pharmacists 73–4
human immunodeficiency virus *see*
  HIV
hyoscine 20, 45
  as antiemetic 34, 37
  in dyspnoea 38, 39
hyoscine-hydrobromide 44
hypercalcaemia 36
hypnotics 43, 45
hypoxia 18, 19

imipramine 33
Indocid R 43
indomethacin 43, 45
insomnia 43, 45
Institute of Oncology 103
International Narcotics Control
  Board 84
International Pharmaceutical
  Federation 87
interpersonal skills 71
isolation 12

journals 130

Kaposi's sarcoma 98

Largactil 20, 44
laxatives 39, 40
lethargy 19
Lisa Sainsbury Foundation 106–7,
  111
Local Authority Social Services 6
lorazepam 20, 34, 37

Macmillan cancer care units 4
Macmillan nurses 101–2
Macmillan Nursing Service 5, 101–2
Macmillan Palliation in Advanced
  Cancer (MacPac) 128
Marie Curie Cancer Care 102–3, 111
  home care services 5
Marie Curie Memorial Foundation
  5, 102–3
Marie Curie Nursing Service 103
Marie Curie Research Institute 103
Maxolon *see* metoclopramide
meningitis, in AIDS 98
MEREC, *Care of the Dying* 66
methadone 58
  control of 76
methotrimeprazine 19, 34, 44
  compatibility with diamorphine
    57
methylcellulose 19
metoclopramide 34, 37
  compatibility with diamorphine
    57
metronidazole gel 66
Misuse of Drugs Act 75
Misuse of Drugs (Notification of and
  Supply to Addicts) Regulations
  1973 77
Misuse of Drugs Regulations 1985
  75
models of care 2, 3, 4
morphine 28, 29, 50–2
  action in CNS 29–30
  control of 76
  in dyspnoea 38, 39
  formulations 50
  preparations 52–3
morphine-6-glucuronide 57

Motor Neurone Disease Association 106, 111
mouth
  dry 19
  problems in AIDS 97
  sore 46, 115–16
MS Contin 88
MST tablets *see* Continus

naproxen (Naprosyn) 28, 31
Narphen 28, 76
National Association of Health Authorities and Trusts 73–4
nausea 33–6
naxolone 29
nebulisation therapy 67–8
networks, international 87
Neuberger, Julia, *Caring for Dying People of Different Faiths* 17
neurotransmitter receptors, in vomiting 33–4
night sweats 43
nitrazepam 45
non-steroidal anti-inflammatory drugs 30, 31
  formulations 49
non-verbal communication 71–2
Normison 45
Nozinan *see* methotrimeprazine
NSAIDs 30, 31
  formulations 49
nursing model of care 2
nystatin (Nystan/Nystavescent) 39

oil retention enema 40
ondansetron 36
Open University 127
opioid analgesics
  action in the CNS 29–30
  availability 83–4
  classification 29
  dependence risks 58, 85
  in dyspnoea 38, 39
  formulations 49–50
  parenteral administration 126
  pharmacological properties 29
  risk of illicit use 84–5

  tolerance to 85–6
opioid receptors 29
Oradexon 39
oral thrush 39
Oramorph 52, 76
oxycodone 28, 76
oxygen, in dyspnoea 38

pain 24–6
  acute 26
  affective component 25
  assessment 27–8, 113–14
  breakthrough 65
  chronic 26–7
  cognitive component 25
  control *see* analgesia
  incidence 82
  mental 30
  physical 26–30
  rational treatment 59
  social 30
  spiritual 32
  tolerance of 26
  WHO programme on relief 83, 131–2
pain threshold 25–6
Palfium 28, 76
palliative care 9–11, 21–47
Palliative Care Distance Learning Programme 129
Palliative Care Programme xi
paracetamol 28, 30, 31, 50, 51
Parker Micropump 54, 55, 56
patients, reactions and fears 12–13
pentamidine 97
pentazocine 28–9, 45
  control of 76
persistent generalised lymphadenopathy, in AIDS 94
pethidine 28
  control of 76
PGL, in AIDS 94
pharmaceutical wholesalers/ manufacturers 66
Pharmacia Deltec CADD pca 54, 55, 56
pharmacists, role of 46

phenazocine 28, 76
phenothiazines 34, 37
phenytoin 45
phosphate enema 40
pneumonia
   in AIDS 97
   in terminal cancer 18
poloxamer 40
prescriptions, for controlled drugs
   76–7, 78
primary care team
   challenges to 6–7
   communication within 72
   interaction with community
      pharmacist 69
Primperan *see* metoclopramide
prochlorperazine 34, 37
progressive multifocal
   leucoencephalopathy 98
Proladone 28, 76
protozoan disease, in AIDS 97
psychotropic drugs 45
pulmonary system, in terminal
   cancer 18
pyridoxine 37

refusal of treatment 15–16
relatives, protectiveness 11–12
renal system, in terminal cancer 18
respiratory system, in AIDS 96, 97
restlessness 19
Retrovir R 95
Roxanol 88
Royal College of General
   Practitioners, Terminal care
   information folder 129

sadness 30
St Christopher's Hospice 1
Scopolamine *see* hyoscine security,
   of controlled drugs 79
sedatives
   as antiemetics 34, 37
   in confusion 42
semi-coma 19
separation anxiety 13
Serenace *see* haloperidol

Sevredol 52, 53, 76, *see also*
   morphine
Single Convention on Narcotic
   Drugs 84
skin conditions, in AIDS 98
Social Services 6
social workers 6
   role of 104–5
spiritual factors 24
SRM-Rhotard 52, 76
Stemetil 34, 37
steroids, in dyspnoea 38
stupor 19
Sue Ryder Foundation 5, 103–4, 111
sulphonamides 45
symptoms
   in AIDS, control 95–9
   in terminal cancer 10, 23
      control 21–46
Synflex 28, 31

temazepam 45
Temgesic *see* buprenorphine
terminal illness, philosophy of 9–20
terminal patients, identification in
   the community 64–5
Terrence Higgins Trust 109
thioridazine 44
training 127–30
tranquillisers 38, 39
treatment, refusal of 15–16
trifluoperazine 44
trimipramine 33

United States, hospice pharmacy 88
   –9
unorthodox therapies 16
uraemia 18, 36
urinary incontinence 46, 117
urinary retention 19

Valoid *see* cyclizine
video tapes 131–2
vitamin B_6 37
voice tone 72
vomiting 21, 33–6

WHO
  Action Programme on Essential
    Drugs 86
  Collaborating Centres 87
  Model List of Essential Drugs 86

  programme on cancer pain relief
    83, 133–4

zidovudine 95